GM Automatic Overdrive Transmission

Builder's and Swapper's Guide

Cliff Ruggles

CarTech®

CarTech®

CarTech,® Inc.
6118 Main Street
North Branch, MN 55056
Telephone (651) 277-1200 • (800) 551-4754 • Fax: (651) 277-1203
www.cartechbooks.com

Edited by: Rick Jensen

ISBN 978-1-932494-50-1

Written, edited, and designed in the U.S.A.
Printed in China
15 14 13 12

Title Page:
Transmission rebuilding requires a suitable work area. As the transmission is taken apart lay the parts out on a workbench. Pay close attention to the order in which they were removed from the case, and inspect each part for wear or damage.

Back Cover Top Left:
For the 4L60E models, removing the TCC solenoid requires removal of the shift solenoid valve just above it. The solenoid must be removed from the pump, before the pump can be pulled from the case.

Back Cover Top Right:
Once you have your case cleaned, it can be painted to protect the surface from oxidation and corrosion. Make sure to completely degrease the unit with brake cleaner. It also helps to warm it up slightly to help the paint penetrate the surface and dry quickly without runs.

Back Cover Middle Left:
The clutch pack is installed on top of the Belleville plate. Start with a steel plate, then a friction, and alternate steel, friction, steel, friction, ending with the backing plate.

Back Cover Middle Right:
A new wiring harness should be included with any 4L60E rebuild. This ensures that you will not have any wiring troubles inside the transmission pan.

Back Cover Bottom Left:
The use of a high-performance or high-stall-speed torque converter can dramatically improve starting-line performance. The car in the near lane is the author's daily driven street car, which runs 11-second quarter-mile times in full street trim. The transmission is equipped with a custom-built aftermarket torque converter supplied by Continental Torque Converters. It is designed to be very efficient for normal driving.

Back Cover Bottom Right:
Slide the transmission/jack rearward and lower it to working height. Pull the torque converter loose and slide it out. Drain the fluid from the converter as well as the transmission (if not already done).

DISTRIBUTION BY:
Europe
PGUK
63 Hatton Garden
London EC1N 8LE, England
Phone: 020 7061 1980 • Fax: 020 7242 3725
www.pguk.co.uk

Australia
Renniks Publications Ltd.
3/37-39 Green Street
Banksmeadow, NSW 2109, Australia
Phone: 2 9695 7055 • Fax: 2 9695 7355
www.renniks.com

Canada
Login Canada
300 Saulteaux Crescent
Winnipeg, MB, R3J 3T2 Canada
Phone: 800 665 1148 • Fax: 800 665 0103
www.lb.ca

S-A DESIGN

Preface

This manual is written for enthusiasts who enjoy working on their own cars or trucks. The information contained within was derived from many, many years of hands-on experience. My goal is to make available to builders the information to help them build a reliable overdrive transmission. Transmissions seem to have a mystique about them that leads many knowledgeable individuals to carry them off to someone else for repair. Oftentimes a customer will send a unit that gives less than desirable results, and that customer may have been charged excessive prices by the previous "specialist." When it breaks or doesn't work right the people who did the work are seldom eager to lend assistance. Why? They already got their money!

This manual provides vital information to builders to use at their discretion. It will not make up for poor building practices, incorrect assembly, or mismatching components. I advise anyone attempting to build his or her own transmission to take great care in doing so. Not to the point of being afraid of the project, but cautious enough to invest the time, money, and effort required for a good end result. Read and re-read the transmission technical information to become fully familiar with the associated parts and terminology. Take great care in transmission disassembly and inspection. Never take anything for granted. If you find damaged items inside your transmission, try to find out why they failed, and ensure that the correct procedures were followed and parts installed to keep it from happening again. You will find in many cases that the transmission may have not been assembled correctly, especially if someone got there before you. Additionally, many builders will apply a few tricks of their own during overhaul. These tricks may deviate from published information and procedures typically applied to correct transmission rebuilding. By following the modifications included within and closely following the overhaul procedures in the rebuilding manual, factory service manuals, or aftermarket technical publications, virtually anyone can produce a reliable unit.

A few special tools are required to complete assembly. Some can be fabricated; others will have to be purchased. I assume no liability for the misuse of the information contained within and wish all of you willing to forge ahead the best of luck with your new endeavor.

Acknowledgments

To Jim Hand, long-time friend and one of the most dedicated performance enthusiasts that I have ever known. Jim supplied history and basic information on the operation of torque converters, plus tips on how to select a torque converter, and basic torque converter characteristics, with excellent definitions on the popular nomenclature associated with torque converters.

To Kris Abrahamson, of Continental Torque Converters. Kris provided a cut-open torque converter for pictures, and also supplied excellent information on the internal components and how they work.

To my good friend and co-worker Ray Klem, for always being there to lend a helping hand.

And to my wife, Debbie, for the many long hours spent on the project, and setting up and shooting photos, and most importantly, putting up with me for 27 years!

Introduction

Modern technology has left us with some good transmission choices for upgrading vintage muscle cars and classics. In the early 1980s, increasingly stringent EPA (Environmental Protection Agency) standards, along with the public's demand for better fuel economy and longer engine life, prompted the major manufacturers to begin the development and production of overdrive transmissions. The first two units were base transmissions already in production: the 700-R4/4L60, based on the TH350, and the 200-4R, a spin-off of the 200-metric transmission. This publication focuses on the 700-R4/4L60 and the later electronically controlled 4L60E. The 4L60E shares most of the common components with the exception of the valve body and lack of a governor and throttle valve, with shifts controlled by the vehicle's Electronic Control Module (ECM).

The 700-R4 transmission began as a light-duty unit available in a variety of vehicles. In addition to a 30-percent overdrive, it employed a lock-up torque converter that ceased torque multiplication once certain driving conditions were met. Lock-up torque converters had already been in service in several General Motors transmissions. A clutch was added to the inside of the torque converter to provide positive engagement between the engine's flywheel and transmission's input shaft. It proved to be a great idea, and further reduced engine RPM and any other associated power losses from the torque converter.

For the first several years of production, the 700, or 4L60, shared the same input-shaft spline as its 200 cousins. Reliability (or lack of it) prompted General Motors to change the converter/pump and input shaft to a much sturdier design. Pump problems continued to plague the 4L60, and several other modifications followed to increase pump, front seal, and torque-converter reliability. In the early years they were still plagued with problems, and several other design changes and upgrades were employed to increase the reliability of the transmission. This book covers these changes and other upgrades that can be performed by the builder to dramatically increase the performance and reliability of the transmission.

This book was written to help the builder in disassembly, inspection, and reassembly of the unit. Since these transmissions received many upgrades and minor design changes, and continued to evolve over years of production, it may not cover all of the factory and aftermarket upgrades that could have been received by specific models and years. Factory service bulletins may cover specific component upgrades and recommended service procedures for different years and models. It is extremely important to correctly identify your transmission by model and year. They are tagged for identification, and I have discussed specific components in this publication to assist the builder. In any and all cases, it is still imperative that the transmission be completely and correctly overhauled, in accordance with the most modern and up-to-date information. Most over-the-counter overhaul/rebuild kits will contain important information, often relating to specific models and changes made to them—which ones may require different check-ball locations or separator-plate gaskets, for example. Aftermarket shift kits contain similar information. Read all of the technical bulletins and other information provided in your rebuild kit and shift kit before rebuilding the transmission.

Transmission rebuilding in general is typically avoided by the average hobbyist and even by most skilled mechanics. Automatic transmissions seem to have a mystique about them that sends even the best-skilled technicians running for cover when the chance to work on one is made available. Most rear-wheel-drive automatics are relatively easy to rebuild and repair, and share many of the same basic components throughout the years of production. Armed with the correct knowledge and a few special tools, they can be easily rebuilt in the home workshop. This book provides the basic information to the reader, along with many tips and special procedures to help make the entire process as easy as possible.

HISTORY

The 700-R4 transmission first came into production in the early 1980s. At the time, emissions standards were tightening and General Motors was hard pressed to increase fuel economy across the board for their production vehicles. Before attempting to integrate an overdrive transmission into their vehicles, the past decade or so had been spent by manufacturers reducing engine displacements and lowering numerical axle ratios to slow the engines down considerably. The aim was to minimize pollutants that exited the tailpipes. The actual end result was dismal overall vehicle performance.

The 700-R4 transmissions received a drastically improved first-gear ratio compared to existing transmissions, most specifically the TH200, TH350, and TH400 (2.74, 2.52, and 2.48, respectively). Moving up to the 3.06 first-gear ratio increased off-idle performance of the vehicles it was installed in considerably. The second-gear ratio was improved to 1.61:1, and third gear remained at 1:1. Some consider the drop from 3.06 to 1.61 a bit steep, but in actual use it is barely noticeable. The 700-R4 transmissions also incorporated a lock-up torque converter to cease all torque multiplication once the TCC (torque converter clutch) was applied. Adding a clutch to the

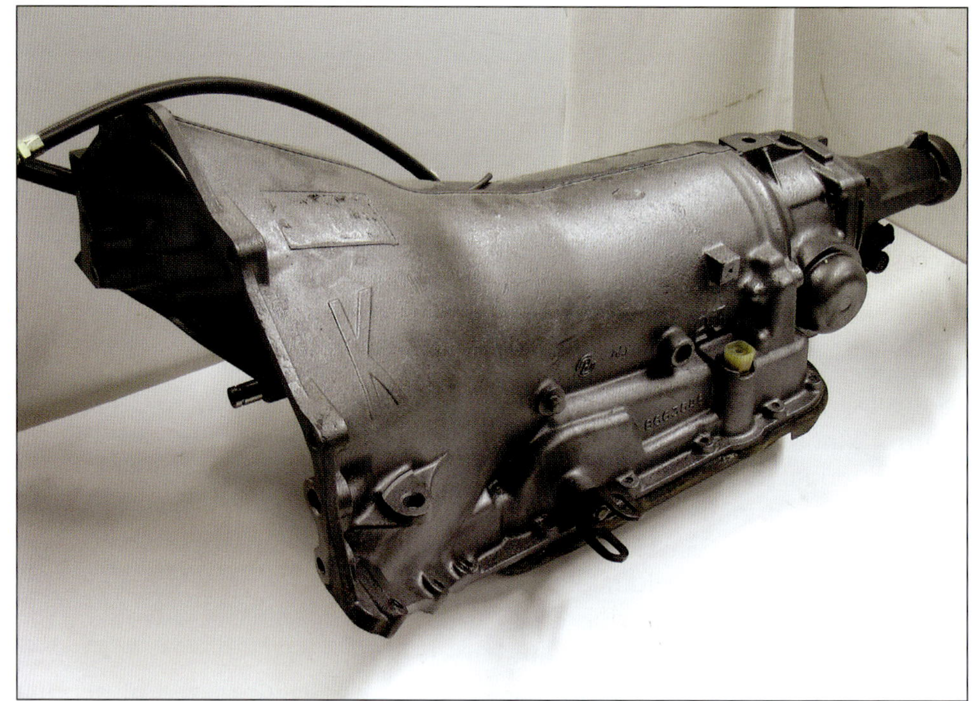

Here is a 4L60 transmission, completely rebuilt and ready to install. This unit was made in or after 1987. The TV cable and governor cover are visible in this view, indicating that it is not a 4L60E unit, which were controlled electronically.

All 4L60 and 4L60E units have a torque converter clutch (TCC) solenoid, located in the oil pump. It could be electronically controlled either by the vehicle's ECM, or by grounding the solenoid on pressure switches located in the valve body. Most units would not allow TCC application until the transmission reached third and/or fourth gear.

Here is a view of a typical wiring harness for a 4L60E transmission with the oil pan removed. Note that this unit uses several switches in the valve body. Shift changes and torque converter clutch (TCC) operation is completely controlled electronically. The 4L60E transmissions will not use a governor or a TV cable. Earlier 4L60 units also used a wiring harness routed through pressure switches to control TCC operation. Even though some later units also provided reference signals to the ECM, shifts were still controlled by reference from the governor and TV cable. Some units also routed the voltage to the TCC through a temperature switch, which would not allow the TCC to employ until the unit was warmed up.

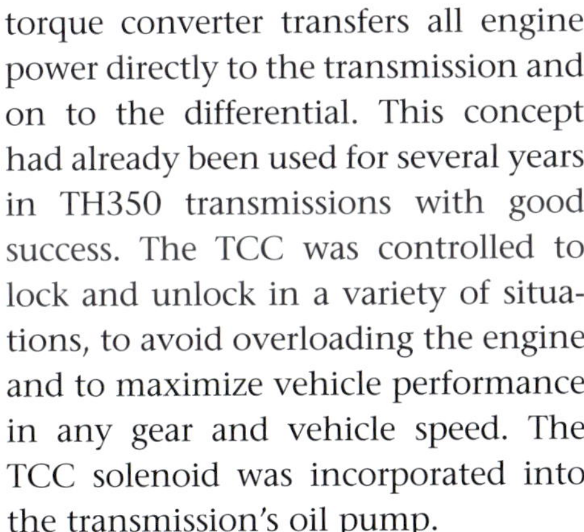

torque converter transfers all engine power directly to the transmission and on to the differential. This concept had already been used for several years in TH350 transmissions with good success. The TCC was controlled to lock and unlock in a variety of situations, to avoid overloading the engine and to maximize vehicle performance in any gear and vehicle speed. The TCC solenoid was incorporated into the transmission's oil pump.

Electrical voltage was supplied to the solenoid to apply the lock-up torque converter by providing a path for high-pressure transmission fluid through the center of the input shaft. An O-ring on the shaft was used to seal inside the torque converter. Several different wiring configurations were used. The voltage to the TCC solenoid was routed through a temperature switch on some models to prevent TCC application until the transmission oil was warmed up. Pressure switches were also used to prevent TCC engagement until the transmission had reached a desired gear. Some units provided TCC application as early as second gear, others not until third or fourth (overdrive).

The 700-R4 transmission also incorporated a .70 ratio fourth gear, or overdrive. This provided a 30-percent reduction in engine RPM once the vehicle attained highway speeds. The extra-low first gear, combined with the .70 overdrive fourth gear, allowed for moderate rear-axle ratios to be used. The improved rear-end gearing and wider selection of transmission ratios made for excellent off-idle performance, low RPM high-speed cruising, and improved performance everywhere in between. The 700-R4 was a great idea, and it quickly replaced the existing TH200 and TH350 transmissions that had been in use for many years.

As with most anything new, the original design was not without flaws. The early unit, made until 1982, used the same small input shaft as its TH200 and 200-4R cousins. The 26-spline input shaft design was quickly upgraded to a larger and stronger 30-spline unit. The original design was made available with several different bell-housing bolt patterns, but for some reason never offered with the BOP (Buick, Oldsmobile, and Pontiac) arrangement. It was, however, made with the standard big-/small-block Chevrolet bell housing, and the 2.8L V-6 pattern.

As General Motors continued production of the 700-R4 transmissions, they expanded its use into heavy-duty applications and several high-performance applications. It found its way into light-duty trucks up to the 2500 designation and behind the relatively stout 305 high-performance engines offered in the Camaros and Firebirds produced in the 1980s and 1990s. Increasing the

Here is a 4L60 case beside a BOP Turbo Hydra-Matic 350 case. The 700s and 4L60/4L60E were never offered with a BOP bell-housing bolt pattern.

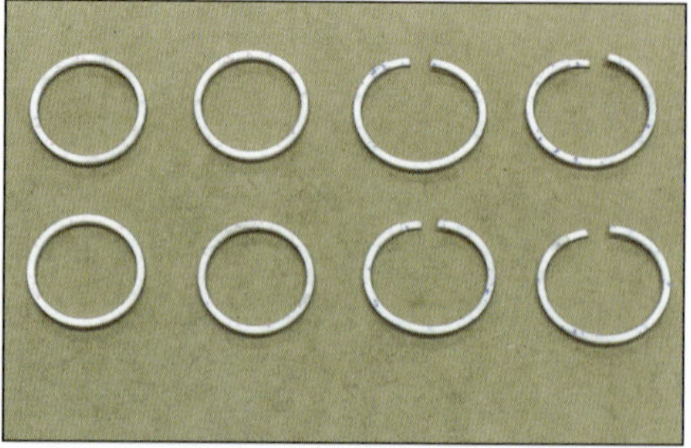

Early units also used scarf-cut Teflon seals at the four locations on the turbine shaft. The solid Teflon seals provided much improved sealing and were a big upgrade for the 4L60 transmissions. Some rebuild kits still come with scarf-cut or interlocking Teflon seals. Always use the solid Teflon seals, even if you have to carry the input drum to a transmission shop to get them installed.

One of the first upgrades given to the 4L60 transmission was an increase in input shaft splines from 26 to 30. Very early units used the same smaller 26-tooth splined input shafts as the smaller 200-4R transmissions.

input torque to the transmission and installing it into heavier vehicles quickly revealed the weak points in the original design. This resulted in the transmission being upgraded several times, and upgrades continued through the years of production.

The end result was an excellent unit. The 700-R4/4L60 transmission became General Motors' workhorse. It was used in nearly every rear-wheel-drive and four-wheel-drive (4WD) vehicle they produced, from the small GMC Jimmys and Blazers, and Camaros and Firebirds, to their entire line of light-duty trucks, and full-size Blazers, Tahoes, and Suburbans.

As mentioned, the first major design change was to increase the input-shaft diameter and number of splines from 26 to 30.

In conjunction with the improved input-shaft change, the factory replaced the scarf-cut turbine-shaft sealing rings with solid rings to improve sealing of the hydraulic fluid flow to the components of the input housing. This greatly improved durability of the forward, 3-4, and overrunning clutch packs, and even more upgrades were yet to come to these areas.

The oil pump also proved to be a fragile point in the transmission, and several pump changes resulted; one was to move up from the original 7-vane design to 10 vanes in 1987. In addition, early units used brittle pump rings; much harder pump rings were incorporated into later units.

Early units were also known for blowing out the front pump seal. This happened mostly because the drain-back hole was not large enough, and fluid flow/pressure from the oil pump would eventually push the seal out of the pump. The

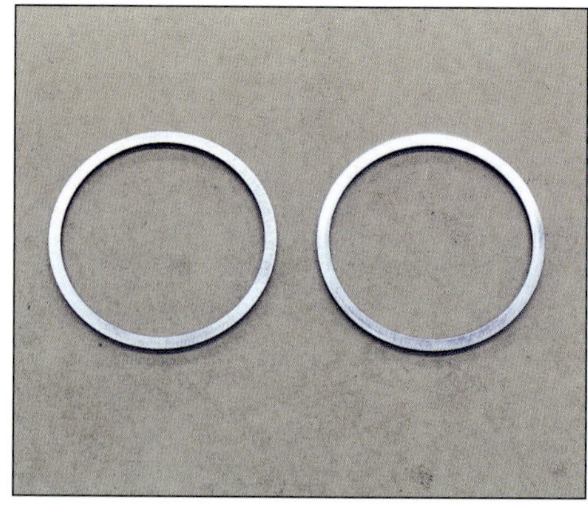

Later 4L60s and 4L60E transmissions used solid Teflon seals on the rear of the pump for the reverse drum. This is another highly recommended upgrade for earlier units.

Very early units developed a quick and bad reputation for blowing out the front pump seal. The factory started adding a retainer to keep the seal in place. The real fix was to increase the diameter of the return oil hole behind the seal. These retainers can be discarded, as they are not needed when the transmission is correctly overhauled.

factory responded by improving the pump design and installing a retainer over the pump seal.

The retainer proved to be not as effective as getting rid of the excess pressure in the first place, but they continued to install the seal retainers through the later years of production. They are not needed on a well-built unit; retaining the seal with red Loctite and making sure the oil drain-back hole is at least 5/16 inch in the passage leading away from the seal will prevent any early seal blowouts due to excessive pressure building up behind it.

Some hard-parts upgrades were also made to the transmissions. Most specifically and important would be replacing any early sun shell with a later or aftermarket hardened unit.

Any 1987-and-later unit will contain the hardened sun shell, even though they may have been used as early as 1986. The stator shafts are

Prior to 1987, the 4L60 may have contained "soft" internal hard parts. Early units were well known for ripping all the teeth off of the inner portion of the sun shell that mated to the sun gear.

also known to be soft, and any rebuild should include a hardened unit, even though 1987-and-newer stator shafts were hardened.

It never hurts to make sure your high-performance transmission has the best possible parts installed for durability. The year 1987 also brought several other major upgrades.

The center-support low/reverse clutch-roller sprag was replaced with a

Early stator shafts were also "soft," which is another problem area that should be addressed during rebuilding. Even on later units that used hardened stator shafts, replace the stator if the splines show signs of wear on the teeth, as with the stator in the picture.

Units made in and after 1987 used a larger and stronger low/reverse sprag. This increased the holding power and durability of the unit. These larger sprag assemblies can be used in the Turbo Hydra-Matic 350 transmissions, although few other parts will interchange.

much stronger unit. The new sprag used longer rollers for more holding power. The later design should be used in all high-performance rebuilds. It's also important to note here that the later 700-R4 and 4L60 heavy-duty sprags and center supports will work in all TH350 transmissions.

The aftermarket has available a heavy-duty bolt-in case saver for the 700s/4L60s, which can be used in a TH350 transmission as well. The bolt-in case savers are relatively inexpensive and a great improvement for the strength of the 700 transmissions.

All TH350s, 700s, and 4L60s are known for excessive wear at the case lugs where they are engaged by the center support. The bolt-in case saver uses case lugs above the retaining snap ring, bolts the two parts together, and increases the strength in that area at least 100 percent.

The OD (overdrive) sprag was also redesigned. Early units used a 26-element "dog"-type sprag clutch. The later unit used a 28-element

The aftermarket offers a bolt-in center support. These units are available with the larger 1987-and-later sprag assemblies, and will also work in TH350 transmissions. Using one is highly recommended for high-horsepower applications, or for any unit that shows considerable wear at the case lugs.

design with its own retainer. This eliminates the need for a thrust washer to be installed on the front of the front planetary. A thrust washer is required to locate the sprag if the early type sprag is used, although using one is not recommended. The later, stronger sprag assembly is a drop-in replacement for all early units.

The reverse drum would also receive a design change. Early units used a steel apply piston. Later, those in and after about 1987 would receive an aluminum apply piston. The aluminum piston has a bleed hole in the piston and is of the feed/bleed design. A large, cupped apply steel is used to soften engagement into reverse, which is a common complaint with these units.

Here is an early (left) and late (right) overdrive sprag, side by side. The early unit contained 26 elements, and required a thrust washer on the front planetary gear. The later unit used 28 elements (most replacement sprags contain 29 elements), and a built-in retainer so that a thrust washer was not needed.

The accumulators for the 1-2 and 2-3 shifts were also redesigned, and the Teflon solid sealing rings were replaced with a rubber seal for improved sealing. The accumulators are used to help control shift performance by increasing the amount of time required to completely apply the clutch packs, or servo, that applies the band. It is a common practice to block off or disable the accumulators to improve shift feel. This can be incredibly hard on the transmission's internals. Accumulators are best left operational. Some of the better shift kits will come with stronger accumulator springs to improve shift feel without transferring undue shock to the hard parts during the shift.

The low planetary assembly would get an oil slinger added to it around 1987. This improves lube flow to the planetary needle bearings. The planetary should be carefully inspected during rebuilding. It is quite common to find excessive endplay at the pinions, requiring replacement of the unit.

To improve 3-4 shift performance, the factory started using a 3-4 apply piston with molded inner and outer seals. This greatly improved 3-4 shift performance and durability. Other changes were made to the overrunning, forward, and 3-4 clutch packs. Early units made until midyear 1987 used thinner friction plates for the forward and overrunning clutch packs. There were also several different arrangements used to stack the drum. Several improvements were made to the 3-4 clutch-pack assembly and the parts used to apply and hold the steels and frictions. The aftermarket also stepped

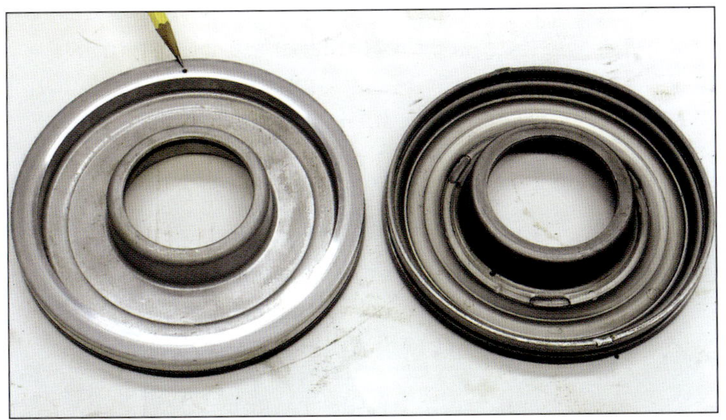

The 1987 and later 4L60s used an aluminum apply piston for the reverse drum. The earlier models used a steel apply piston. These parts are not interchangeable, as other modifications to the transmission were made to effectively use the "feed/bleed" system in the later drum with the aluminum apply piston.

Very early accumulators (left) used Teflon sealing rings. These designs were replaced with a later piston that used a rubber seal for more effective sealing. Accumulator pistons may also develop excessive wear in the center where they slide on the pin. This may cause poor or delayed shifting, and early clutch-pack failure. Always use the later style pistons and seals, and make sure there is no excessive wear or play where the pin goes through the piston.

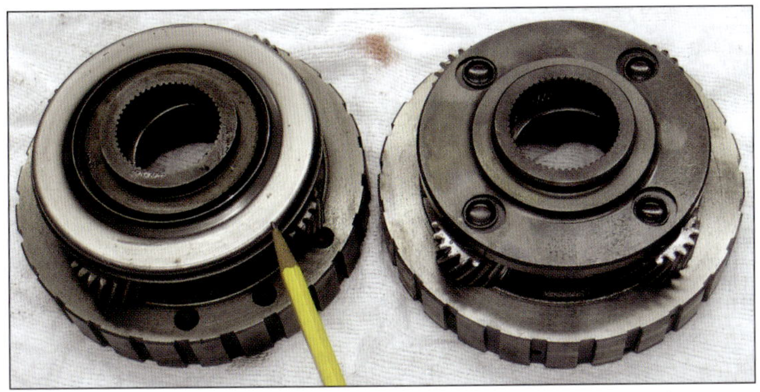

An oil slinger was added to later 4L60 units to improve oiling to the low/reverse planetary gears. The oil slinger is probably not all that effective, as we've seen both early and late high-mileage units suffer considerable wear to the low/reverse planetary assembly. This is an assembly item that is often overlooked. Always check the pinions for rough spots and/or excessive endplay, worn or missing thrust washers, etc.

Another big upgrade for the 4L60s was the implementation of steel apply pistons with molded seals. These pistons replaced the aluminum apply pistons with replaceable rubber lip seals. The molded apply pistons are easier to install, and improve sealing and holding power to the clutch packs when they apply.

in with greatly improved arrangements, as the 3-4 clutch pack has always been a sore spot for these transmissions.

A large band was used for second and fourth gear. The band is installed in the front portion of the case and is designed to grab and hold the reverse drum. The reverse drum is made from stamped steel and is extremely slippery. It became a tall order for the band to effectively apply and hold the drum. GM made several changes to the servo and also incorporated valve-body changes to improve performance in this area. The servo that applies the band was offered in several configurations. The inner piston was used to apply the band for second gear. Increasing the diameter of the piston provided additional holding power. This not only improved durability but shift performance as well. The first improved bands were offered in early Corvette applications. The Corvette servo can be installed into any unit. The aftermarket also stepped up with even larger diameter servo assemblies.

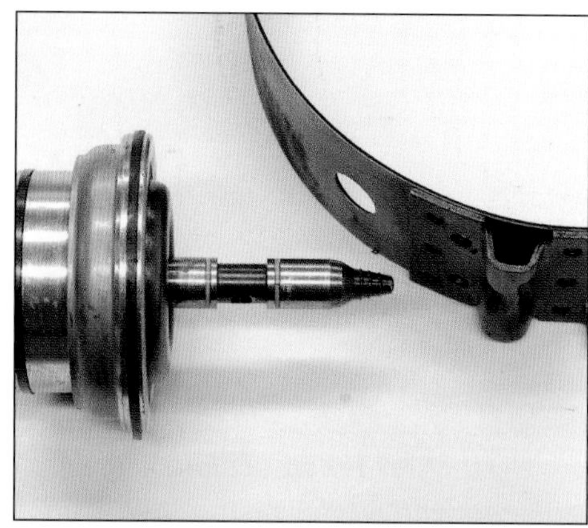

A servo assembly was used to apply the band for the 1-2 and 3-4 shifts. Several different sizes of servos were used. The largest pistons were used on the Corvette, and a few other heavy-duty truck and passenger-car applications.

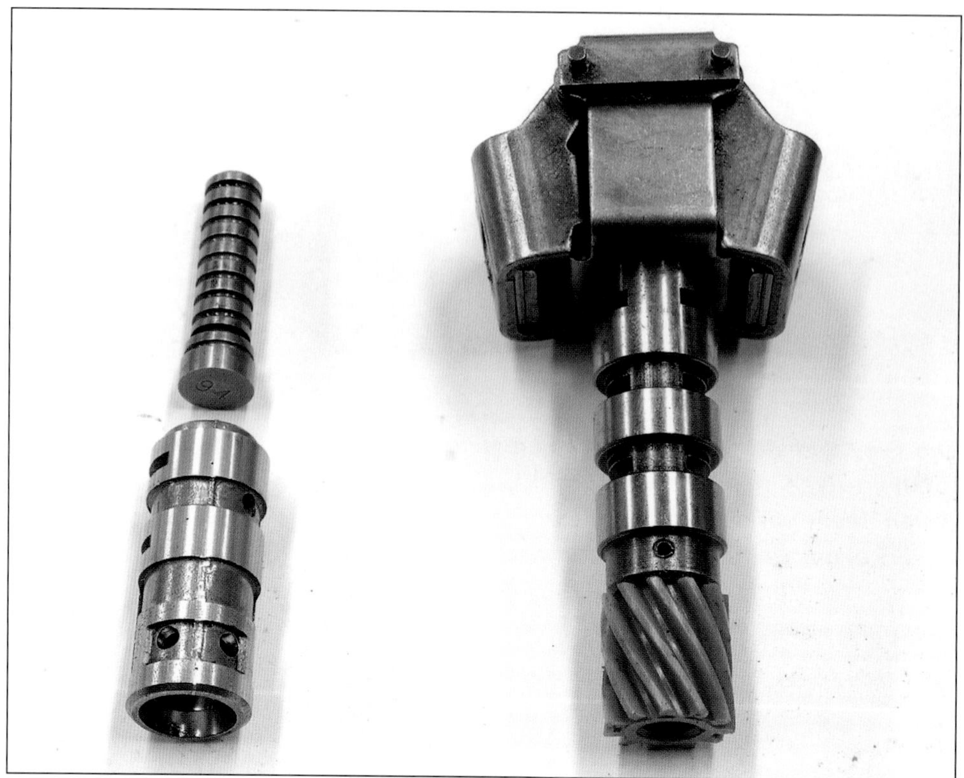

All models prior to the introduction of the 4L60E used a governor and throttle valve (TV) to control all shifts. The throttle valves used in early units were known to stick or hang up, causing delayed or late/firm shifts, and in extreme cases complete loss of all upshifts. The factory sleeve and plunger are shown in the picture on the left. A closer view of the sleeve, plunger, and TV valve are shown on the right. Most aftermarket shift kits contain modified components to prevent throttle-valve problems; these items are shown and discussed in Chapter 4.

All 700s through 1992 used a throttle valve to control gear changes. The throttle valve was operated by a cable connected to the carburetor or throttle body, and provided the transmission with a reference point for throttle position. Combined with a governor in the rear of the main case, driven by the output shaft, this provided control of all upshifting and downshifting. The throttle valve was redesigned in the mid 1980s, as the early design was prone to sticking or hanging up and causing loss of, or poor, shift performance. The throttle valve was also designed to prevent high-speed heavy- or full-throttle operation in fourth gear. The 700s used in Corvettes had a specially designed throttle-valve sleeve that allowed fourth-gear operation at heavy- and full-throttle openings. This part can be used in all 700s, if this feature is desired.

By 1987, General Motors had the 700 transmissions beefed up and holding up well in every application in which they were used. If you are looking for a unit to retrofit, or to upgrade an existing unit, it is highly recommended to use a transmission produced after mid-1987. These units are easily identifiable, as the case was redesigned and they have an auxiliary valve body under the pan. The case sports a large casting line, similar in shape to a cam lobe, on the passenger side. The casting line extends up and curves through the cooling-line bosses. These improved units made through 1992 will also have a governor and a TV (throttle valve) cable. This makes installing them into earlier vehicles much easier than installing electronically controlled units. Later electronically controlled cases have the cam-lobe casting, but a big bundle of wires in lieu of the governor and cable. These electronically controlled units started showing up in 1992 and replaced the earlier units by 1993.

Electronic units are basically the same internally as for hard parts, but completely different in the valve-body area. They are fully computer controlled and difficult to retrofit into older vehicles without purchasing expensive special components. To retrofit any non-computer-controlled unit, all the installer has to do is modify the carburetor's primary throttle shaft with a provision to attach the TV cable. No vacuum modulator is used on any of the early 700s. All shifts are controlled by throttle position (TV cable) and vehicle speed (governor).

The electronically controlled 4L60E units continued to receive minor upgrades through the years of production. These included a 13-vane pump. Increasing the number of vanes does not improve pump output but does smooth out the pulsations and is said to improve pump life. Any of the later 10- or 13-vane pumps can be installed into earlier pump housings to replace the 6-vane units. The transmission case also received a major upgrade in the late 1990s. The case was modified for a removable bell housing. This greatly increased the strength of the transmission where the bell housing attaches to the case. GM had always had some issues with case failures, especially with 4WD applications. The additional weight and flexing imposed on the transmission from the transfer case had always been a problem area. Adding a removable bell housing was a great improvement for these applications.

Overall, the 700/4L60 transmission has been a great success for General Motors. Despite getting a bad reputation from the early versions, the transmission proved to be a very durable and reliable unit. With the ever-increasing cost of fuel, retrofitting these transmissions into early vehicles has become increasingly popular. When correctly prepared, they have proven themselves to be extremely durable, and will provide the user with the very best of both worlds—amazing starting-line performance from the 3.06 first-gear ratio, and a 30-percent reduction in engine speeds when cruising in overdrive.

Here is a great salvage yard find, a 1987 or later 4L60. Note the cam lobe shaped parting line, and provision for the TV cable. If the valve body were removed from this unit we will also find an oil tube from the pump to an auxiliary valve body. Early models do not have this cam lobe shaped parting line on the case, or the auxiliary valve body under the oil pan. They will not contain all of the factory upgrades, but can be built to the later specifications with some additional cost.

Pictured here is a 1998 case showing the removable bolt on the bell housing. Later units were made with a bolt-on bell housing. These units are stronger than early designs, which were known for occasional failure in some heavy-duty applications, especially in 4WD vehicles where a heavy transfer case is bolted to the end of the transmission.

CHAPTER 2

GETTING STARTED

Safety Equipment

Rebuilding a transmission, like most other shop-related activities, can expose the rebuilder to certain safety hazards. The most common for transmission rebuilding is exposure to petroleum-based oils, solvents, and other chemicals. Nitrile gloves, similar to latex gloves used by hospital personnel, will protect the user from many chemical hazards. They also help to protect the hands from being cut by sharp components, such as machined-out areas inside the transmission case. Blowing compressed air into tiny passages creates very high-pitched sounds, and combined with the pounding of a hammer to remove or replace bearings, it can damage hearing. Hearing protection should be worn anytime you would be exposed to loud noises. You will also need to protect your eyes from flying debris and the possibility of solvents or transmission fluid getting into them. I can't think of anything that burns your

Nitrile gloves protect hands from petroleum products and solvents used to clean the transmission. Safety glasses are inexpensive; several varieties are shown, and the ones with the side shields are preferred. Hearing protection should be used when banging, pounding, or blowing out the case passages with compressed air.

Several different styles of transmission-holding fixtures are available. The holder on the top was designed specifically for General Motors automatic transmissions. The holder on the bottom is universal, and attaches to the pan rail using longer bolts. Either type works equally well, and allows the transmission to be flipped around and locked into various positions.

Two casting lugs are on all 700, 4L60, and 4L60E cases to accommodate the special holding fixture designed for GM transmissions.

eyes more than automatic transmission fluid. Safety glasses with side shields are highly recommended.

There may be inhalation hazards associated with using chemical solvents. Some may also be flammable. Read the warning labels on the cans for specific guidance, always work in a well-ventilated area, and make sure that there are no appliances in the immediate work area that have a pilot light.

A Place to Work

In order to successfully rebuild a transmission, a suitable workplace and an assortment of tools are required. Due to the complexity of a transmission, a clean, dirt- and dust-free environment is necessary. Any dust and dirt that find their way into the transmission can, and probably will, cause function issues when the unit is placed in service. It is a good idea to purchase a few large 55-gallon heavy-duty trash bags. They can be used to cover the transmission tightly between rebuilding sessions. This will help to ensure that nothing finds its way into the unit if it sits on the bench for a few days while being rebuilt.

A large worktable or workbench makes a great place to lay out all the components of the transmission during rebuilding. It should be large enough to hold the transmission and

The universal transmission-holding fixture works well, but the fixture will have to be removed to install the transmission oil pan.

all of its components, and the parts from the rebuild kit. Although not mandatory, a fixture to hold the unit in suspension from the workbench will make the unit much easier to take apart and re-assemble.

Several different types of transmission-holding fixtures are available, including ones made especially for General Motors units. Through the years of production, GM was kind enough to cast into the cases two attachment points designed for a special holding fixture.

Several companies also make universal tools designed to attach through the pan bolts.

Although not quite as desirable as the GM-style fixture, they will securely hold the unit and allow it to be rotated to different positions to facilitate removal and re-installation of the internals.

In lieu of not having a suitable holding fixture for the transmission, a small wooden box with a hole in the center to accommodate the output shaft will act as a stand for the transmission during assembly. The box can be drilled to accommodate several of the tail-housing bolts, to keep it from falling over while the parts are being stacked into the unit. You can also use an old aluminum bell housing to hold the unit up off the floor. The hole through the center of the bell housing accommodates the output shaft, while the flat surface of the rear portion of the transmission sits on the flat lower portion of the bell housing.

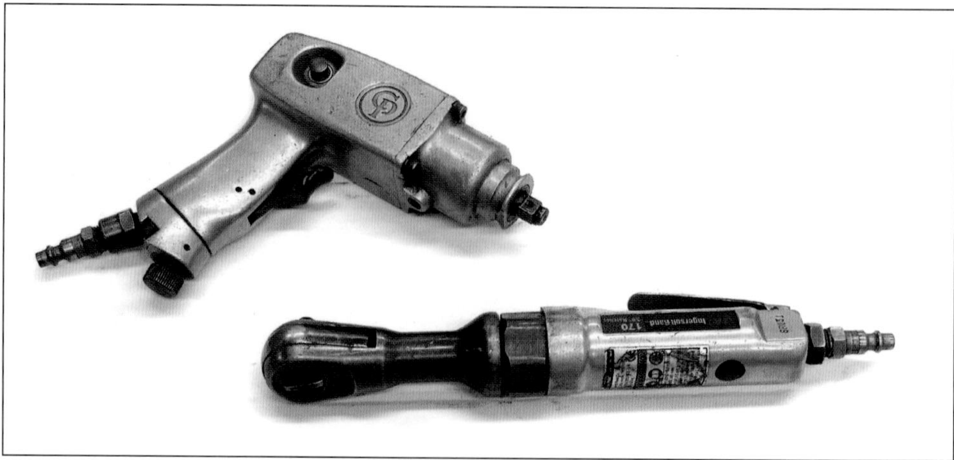
Air tools will cut down disassembly time considerably. They should not be used to assemble the transmission, due to the possibility of stripping out bolts in the aluminum case.

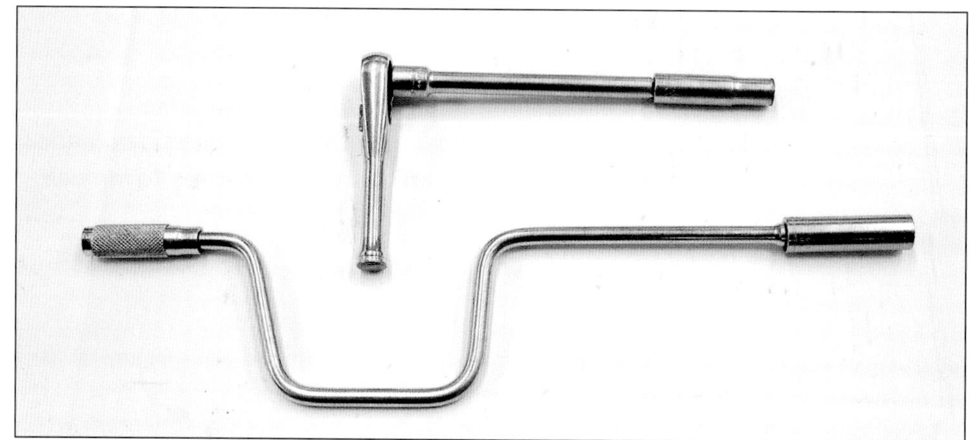
A speed handle will help cut down time installing the many fasteners holding down the oil pan and valve body. Use a modified ⅜-in-drive ratchet to tighten the oil-pan bolts. Over-tightening can lead to stripped threads.

Air Tools

Rebuilding a transmission will require compressed air. Even if air tools are not used, compressed air is needed to air check the function of various components to ensure they are correctly assembled. Compressed air can be used to apply clutch packs, and the servo for the band. Any air leaks will indicate that the component is not sealing correctly. This must be corrected before the unit is placed in service. Any air leaks will allow pressurized transmission fluid to leak by lowering the hydraulic pressure and the needed apply force to the components to be checked.

Air tools also prove helpful to speed up the time required to rebuild the transmission, but are not mandatory. A ⅜-in-drive air wrench, or small ⅜-in-drive air-impact wrench, will save time removing the many bolts holding down the valve body and other components.

Even so, it should not be used to reassemble the transmission, as many of the small bolts are easily broken off in the case, and the possibility also exists of stripping the aluminum threads out of the case. A speed-handle wrench is a much better choice for installing bolts, followed by careful final tightening with a ratchet. In addition to an air ratchet, a 90-degree angle grinder outfitted with abrasive disks will come in handy to clean stuck gasket material on the pan and other flat, machined surfaces of the transmission.

Care must be taken, however, when using abrasive disks to clean gasket material from the lower portion of the case where the valve-body separator-plate gaskets seal. The abrasive disks can leave "tracks" in the aluminum, and cause cross flowing of transmission fluid when it is under pressure. The steel separator plate should also be carefully cleaned of gasket material. Avoid using any tools that will mar the surface and prevent effective sealing between the parts.

An air blowgun will also be required. The variety with the long, curved tube works the best for transmission work. In addition to blowing out small passages during the cleaning process, the tube can be inserted into fluid-supply passages to air check apply pistons in the clutch packs, and the low/reverse apply piston in the case.

During the rebuilding process, all components will be air-checked for proper function. Some can be checked on the bench, others only while in the case. Air checking is important, and all components must pass the air test before the unit is placed in service. Some components can be checked on the bench, and in the case, and others both before and after the transmission is assembled.

In order to keep many of the small parts from falling onto the floor a large, flat pan or cookie sheet is desirable. The large cookie sheets are available at most food supply wholesalers and retailers.

It's best to have several cookie sheets available, one for the valve body and all the check balls, and another one for the clean assembly work of various other components.

Compressed air is needed to check the function of the clutch packs. It can also be used to remove the low/reverse piston by applying air to the case, as shown in this picture.

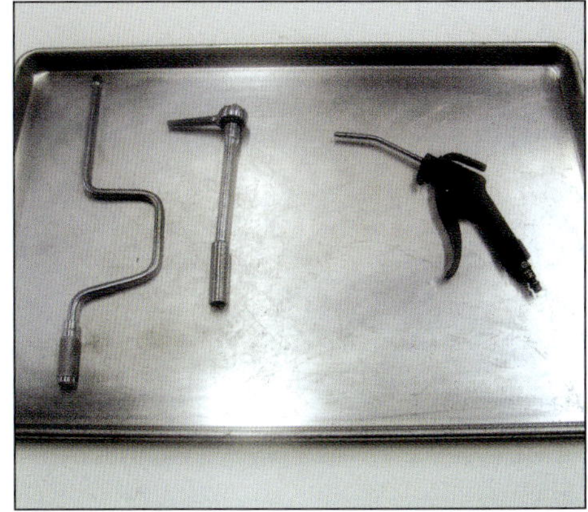

Large commercial cookie sheets are great for placing the valve body and other small parts in, to ensure they don't end up on the floor. They are made of aluminum and are very inexpensive.

Since a transmission is a complex hydraulic system, cleanliness is of the utmost importance. All parts should be thoroughly cleaned and degreased, starting with the transmission case. Typically, the inside of the case will be very clean, unless the transmission was overheated due to

Most machine shops have the ability to hot tank the case, and it is well worth the additional time and expense. The case will come back cleaned inside and out, and after a quick spray with brake cleaner and a blow off, it is ready to assemble.

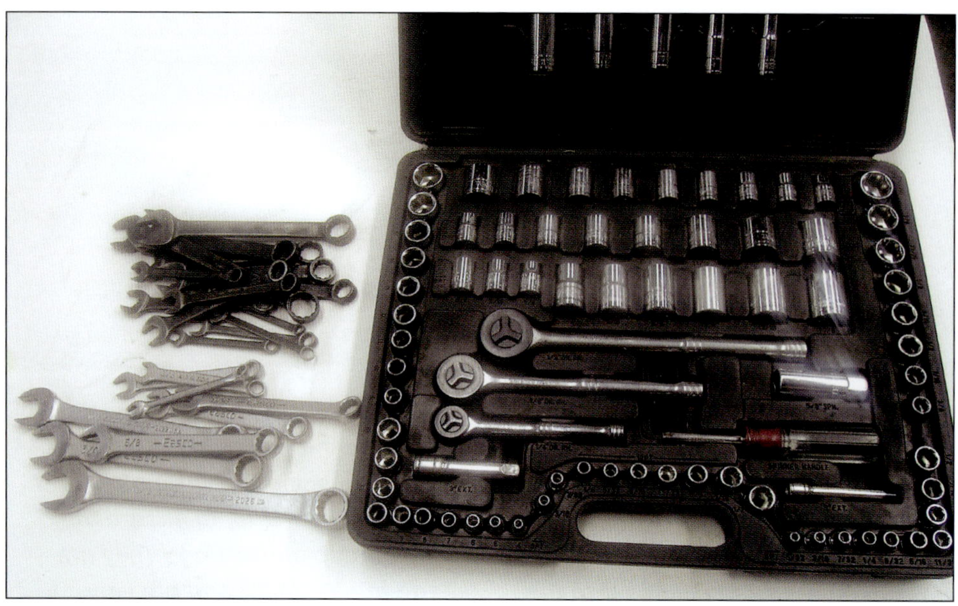

A good ⅜-in and ¼-in drive socket set is needed for taking the transmission apart. Six-point sockets are preferred, as they lessen the likelihood of rounding off the bolt heads on some of the tiny fasteners for the valve body. Metric wrenches will be needed to loosen the manual shaft nut and one of the bolts on the tail housing below the speedometer drive.

A small flat-tip screwdriver will prove invaluable for checking the movement of valves in the valve body. A magnetic tip on the handle is also handy for removing the steel check balls from the case passages under the separator plate.

Engine spray cleaner can be used to pre-soak the case if you are going to clean it at home. This helps soften up and remove much of the heavy grease and dirt. Several other heavy-duty degreasing chemicals can be purchased at local auto parts stores. The "purple" cleaner shown also works great on cleaning up the shop floor.

excessive clutch-pack or band slippage. The outside of the case is usually just the opposite, and may be heavily soiled with grease, grime, undercoating, etc. It may be money well spent to drop the case off at a machine shop for hot tanking.

If cleaning the case at home, a high-pressure washer can be used to remove most of the heavy deposits. Scrapers and wire brushes may be required for some of the more stubborn areas. Regardless of the cleaning method, the transmission case should be spot-free inside and out, as the smallest particle of debris that gets into the unit can cause troubles once the transmission is placed in service.

Carburetor and brake-parts spray cleaners also work well to help clean and degrease the inside and outside of the case. It is preferable to use brake cleaner on the valve body and other internal components, as it dries grease and oil free.

Hand Tools

For most of the transmission-rebuilding operation, a good socket set and a few common hand tools are all that will be needed. The fasteners in the 700s are metric, or Torx drive. A basic ¼-in through ⅜-in socket set, preferably with 6-point sockets and a heavy-duty set of Torx drive sockets, will be needed.

A metric box/open end wrench set will also be needed. A good assortment of flat tip screwdrivers will also come in handy; especially a very small one. A small screwdriver is needed to test the operation of the various valves in the valve body.

A small awl is also great at removing the snap-ring retainer on the 2-4 servo cover, and can also be used to pry out the input-shaft check ball/capsule if needed.

Several hammers will also be required: machinist's hammers; one

An awl can be used to help remove the snap ring for the servo cover.

Snap-ring pliers are invaluable in transmission rebuilding. There are quite a few snap rings holding various components in place. Some can be removed with screwdrivers; others are only accessible using snap-ring pliers.

small and one medium size will be fine. A large leather mallet can be used to help loosen up the servo cover when required. Some cars that have been in a lot of road salt may have enough rust and corrosion around the servo cover to make it difficult to remove. A large soft-faced hammer, rubber or leather, will work best for "shocking" it loose.

A couple of types and styles of snap-ring pliers will also be required.

Some servo covers will be very difficult to remove, especially on cars and trucks that have been driven in the salt. A few taps with a soft-faced hammer, such as the leather mallet shown, will help loosen up the servo cover so it can be removed from the case.

A small reversible pair works great for removing the snap ring retaining the pressure-regulator valve. A large pair is needed for the heavy-duty snap ring on the forward spring cage, and a custom pair will be required to remove the front snap ring on the output shaft, and the snap ring retaining the low/reverse spring cage in the case.

Special Tools

Usually the most apprehensive part of tackling a transmission rebuild is going out and purchasing a lot of special tools. This area of the hobby has for many years scared off even the most skilled hobbyists; even many well-skilled technicians avoid transmission work due to the rumored complexity of the job and having to use a lot of special tools. Yes, some special tools will be required. The good news is that most of them can be easily fabricated, in lieu of spending a lot of money on the ones listed in the various service manuals. About the only two special tools I've never

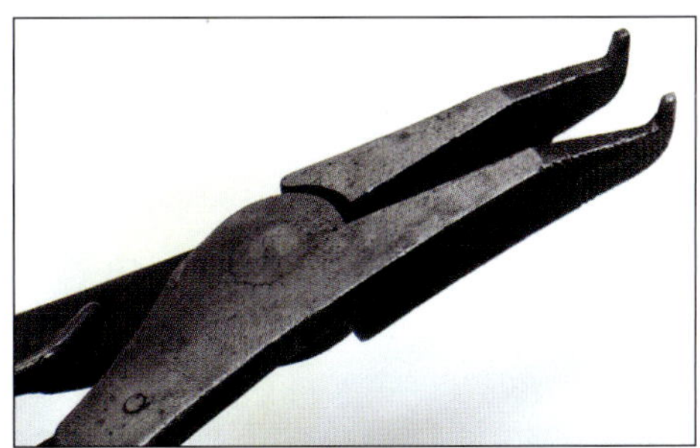

A modified set of snap ring pliers is shown. The wide tips of the tool have been carefully ground to a smaller size. The smaller ends are needed to remove the snap ring from the upper end of the output shaft, and also work well for removing the snap ring holding the low/reverse spring cage in the case.

Of all the tools listed, these are two that are difficult to go without. The installation of solid Teflon sealing rings on the stator and turbine shafts is highly recommended. The tools shown not only install the seals, but also resize them.

If a shop press isn't available, you can fabricate a very effective spring compressor. The one shown in the picture was made from two different sizes of square tubing, at a very minimal cost.

A spring compressor is required to compress the low/reverse spring cage in the lower part of the case. One can be easily fabricated from simple components, as was the one shown in the picture. We have used this compressor for over 25 years, and it has successfully compressed hundreds and hundreds of spring cages. Note the wear on the nut used to tighten the tool.

been able to successfully fabricate are the tools to install the solid stator shaft and turbine-shaft Teflon seals. Some builders use the scarf-cut, or other types of cut, Teflon seals, in lieu of buying the tools to install solid ones. I highly recommend installing solid Teflon seals in both places, since they guarantee a leak-free fit for improved performance and maximum transmission life.

Much like its TH350 cousin, the 700 requires a spring compressor for the low/reverse spring-cage snapring located in the bottom of the case. A simple homemade spring compressor can be fabricated in minutes to successfully accomplish the task. All that is needed are two flat pieces of steel, about 1 in wide and at least ¼ in thick, a piece of hardened all-thread, and hex nuts and washers. I have used an old socket as a spacer for my tool, simply to make it easier to install and remove.

A spring compressor will also be required to rebuild the reverse drum and the turbine-shaft drum. A shop press can be made to work, or you can fabricate a simple spring compressor for the task.

Various types of spring compressors are available, although they are somewhat expensive. Some are bench-top models, but others can also be used in the case as required to compress the spring cage for the low/reverse piston.

I recommend installing a full set of bushings into all rebuilds. This is not always necessary, or mandatory, but guarantees that the transmission will have minimum tolerances, or minimal up/down movement, between all the components when placed in service. Combined with new thrust washers, and the correct selective washer, the transmission will seal up tighter, run quieter, perform better, and last longer. Some bushings can be somewhat difficult or complicated to repair and restore. The best method to remove them is by making a special punch with an angled/sharp end. The sharp angled end will catch the edge of the old bushings and usually quickly remove them.

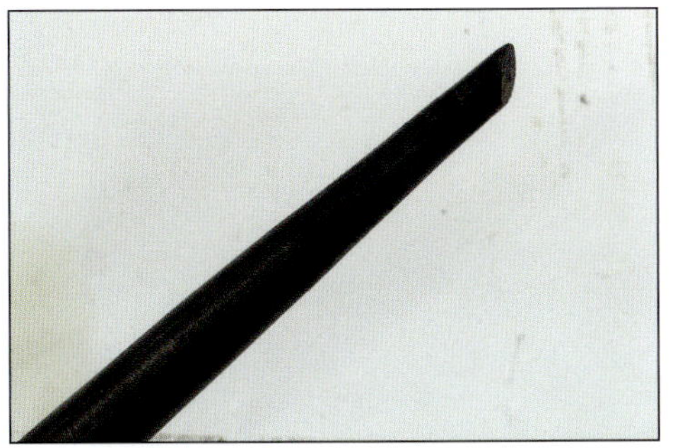

Removing bushings can be challenging. Grinding the end to an angle can modify a long, heavy-duty punch. This allows the punch to more effectively grab and remove the bushings without slipping off. Care must be used not to gouge or scratch the surface of the component under the bushing.

Since most bushings are driven in flush, it's usually pretty easy to find suitable drivers to install them. Some bushings, as noted in the rebuilding section, are "set" below flush, and therefore require the correct diameter driver to correctly install them. This may mean fabricating a driver, or purchasing a bushing-driver set. Both front and rear seals also require a large, flat driver to seat them. Nearly any large, flat material will work: a block of wood, a piece of metal, etc. The best seal driver I have found is an old valve from a large diesel engine.

For decades, most GM transmissions had 3/8-16 threads in at least two of the pump-housing boltholes. This made for easy pump removal with a slide hammer. On 700s, the holes are not tapped. It's really not a big show-stopper, as there is sufficient room under the pump to pry it out of the case with a big, flat screwdriver or pry bar. A 3/8-16 slide hammer is a great tool to remove the check ball/capsule in the case beside the 2-4 servo assembly, if it requires replacement.

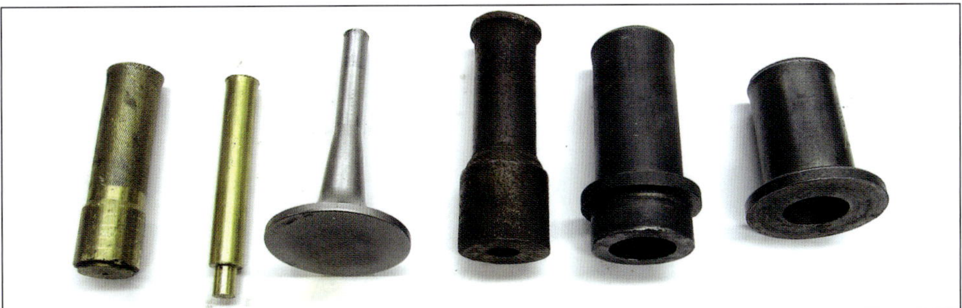

Through the years, I have used quite a variety of components to drive in bushings and seals. Some of them are shown in the picture.

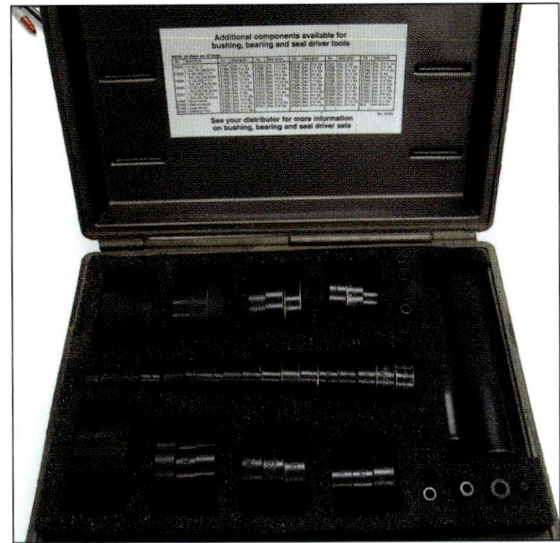

Complete bushing-driver sets are available from several sources. The kit shown here will drive bushings into hard-to-reach places. This kit is made of steel. Lower cost kits using plastic drivers are available and work fine, especially if the builder isn't going to do a lot of transmissions.

A slide hammer can be used to remove the oil pump, if the extra time is taken to tap a couple of the pump holes for 3/8-16 threads. It also makes a great tool to remove the check ball and capsule located next to the servo if it is found to be defective.

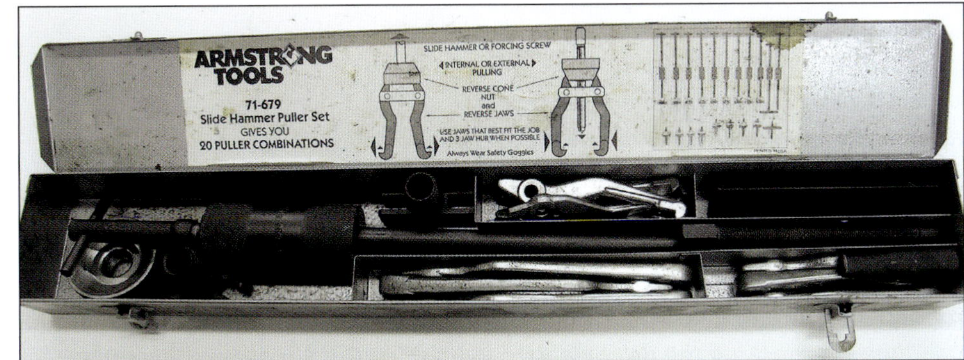

A slide hammer kit can also be used to remove transmission bushings. Some bushings are seated well below the surface, such as the front stator input-shaft bushing. A puller makes removing them much easier.

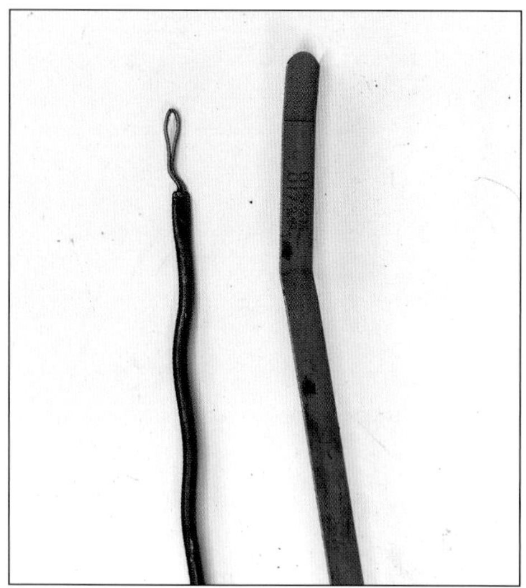

Installing pistons with rubber lip seals can be frustrating. Several companies make special seal-installation tools; they are nothing more than large plastic cups. You can also install pistons having lip seals by making a custom tool from a piece of small copper or steel tubing and a piece of wire, as shown. A long feeler gauge also works if care is taken not to cut the seals during installation. If the apply piston uses a lip-type seal, the lip is always installed facing down, or toward where the pressurized ATF (automatic transmission fluid) will come from. The factory has chamfered all of the drums in the 4L60 and 4L60E transmissions to facilitate the installation of lip-type seals. The seal-installation tools are used to get the edge of the seal lip past the chamfered edge. This is accomplished by running the tool around both the outer and inner seal lips while pushing down gently on the apply piston. Once both the inner and outer lip seals are past the chamfered portion of the drum, the seal can be rotated slightly and gently pushed into position. Air checking the drums and servo is outlined in Chapter 3, to make sure that you have correctly installed your apply piston seals.

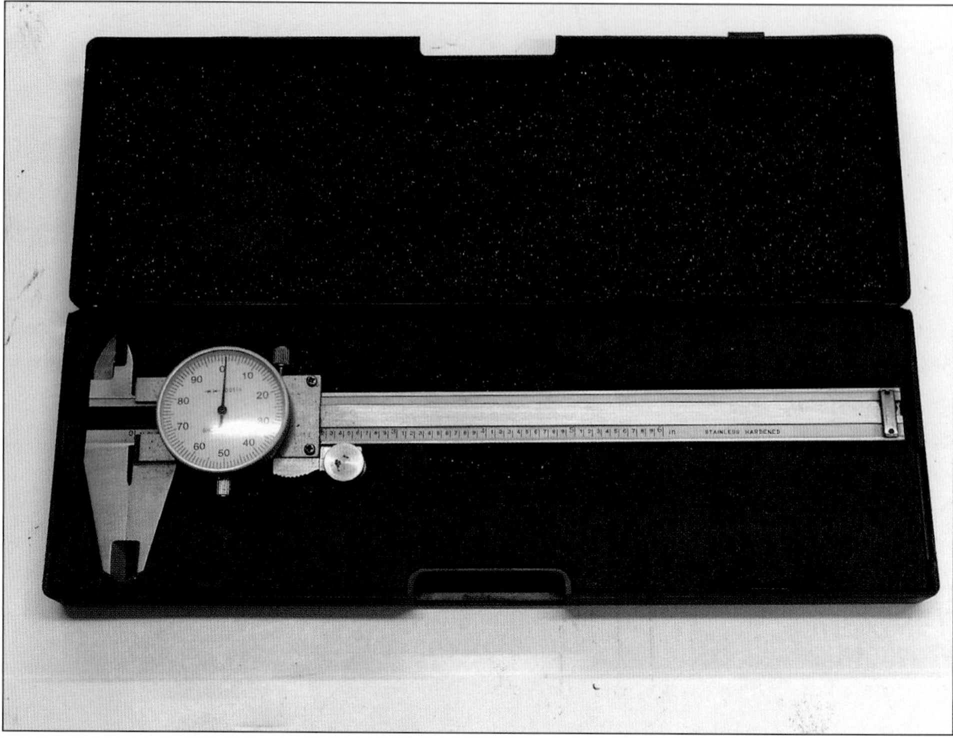

A slide caliper will prove handy to measure steels and friction plates. Several different thicknesses of steels and frictions were used through the years of production, and it is important to check the total thickness of your clutch packs for each drum. The slide caliper also measures depth, and can be used to help set bushings back to their original depth when driving them in.

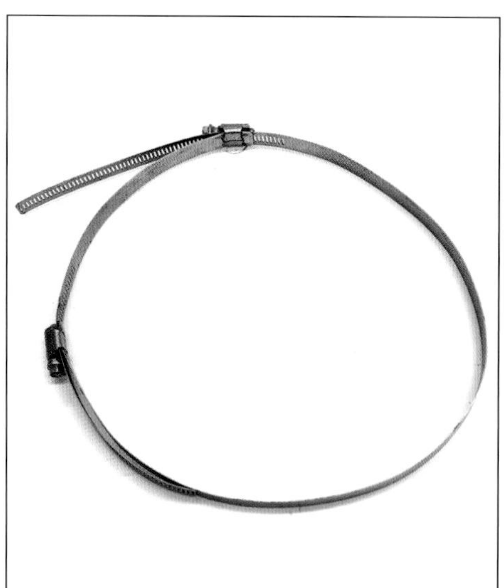

The oil-pump halves will need to be aligned for re-installation into the case. A large stainless-steel hose clamp makes a perfect alignment tool. Several smaller clamps can be put together, which work equally well.

For the more sophisticated builder, several companies market excellent slide hammer kits. They have enough attachments to remove most any stubborn seal or bushing.

Installing lip seals can be accomplished by using a large feeler gauge, or a length of small copper or steel tubing with a piece of small turbine wire crimped in the end. At first installing pistons and lip seals will seem difficult. But with plenty of lubricant and patience the pistons will just about fall into the drums.

You will have to measure several items in the transmission during the rebuilding process. Several different thicknesses of steel and friction plates were used through the years of production. A dial caliper will be needed for determining component

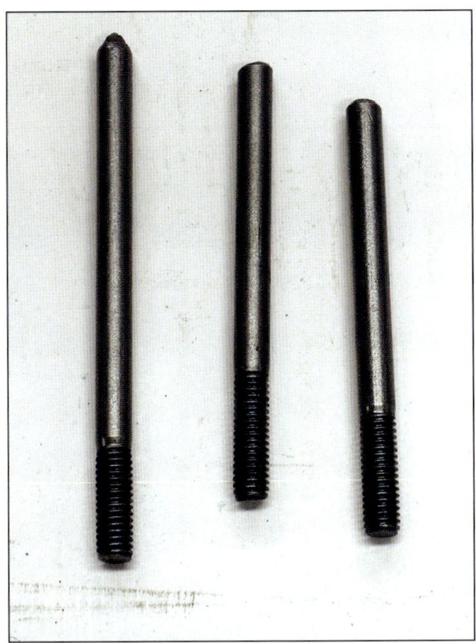

A couple of old pump bolts can be modified to act as guide pins when re-installing the oil pump.

dimensions, and also for total clutch-pack thickness. You can also use the caliper to measure diameters, both inside and outside, and depth, such as how deep a bushing is driven into a particular component. This is for later reference when a new bushing is installed.

You will also need an oil-pump alignment tool after the pump is taken apart for rebuilding. The pump is basically two halves with closely machined tolerances. They must be correctly aligned before being put back into the transmission case. A large stainless-steel hose clamp, or a combination of several smaller clamps, will work fine for this job.

To help guide the oil pump into position on the case, a couple of old pump bolts with the heads removed and the ends ground to a point will make the task much easier.

If you are taking the valve body apart for cleaning, you'll see that small roll pins retain most of the valves. Some shift kits will include a special tool to easily remove the factory roll pins. If not, one can be made from a small piece of flat spring steel, bent at 90 degrees and ground on one end to a sharp point. The tool's sharp point is inserted into the roll pin to spin it free and pull it out.

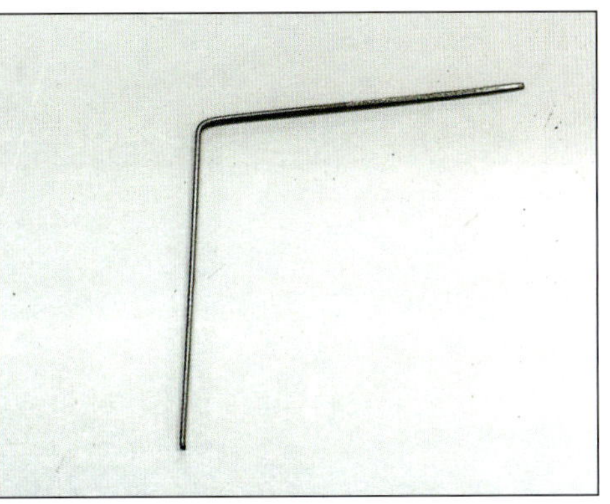

A roll pin removal tool will be needed to remove valves from the valve body, some of which are inserted into "blind" holes. Some shift "kits" will have a tool in them. The tool in the picture is from a Transgo shift kit.

Most screwdrivers will be hardened enough at the end that they will break if you attempt to bend them. Heating them for a few minutes will soften the material enough to allow for easy bending.

Plates Removal

When taking the transmission apart, it can be difficult and time consuming to remove the steel and friction plates from the various drums and clutch packs, especially if you are custom stacking the drum and have to take it apart several times. In lieu of turning the drums upside down and dumping all the components onto the workbench, you can fabricate a couple of screwdrivers to remove the frictions and steel plates.

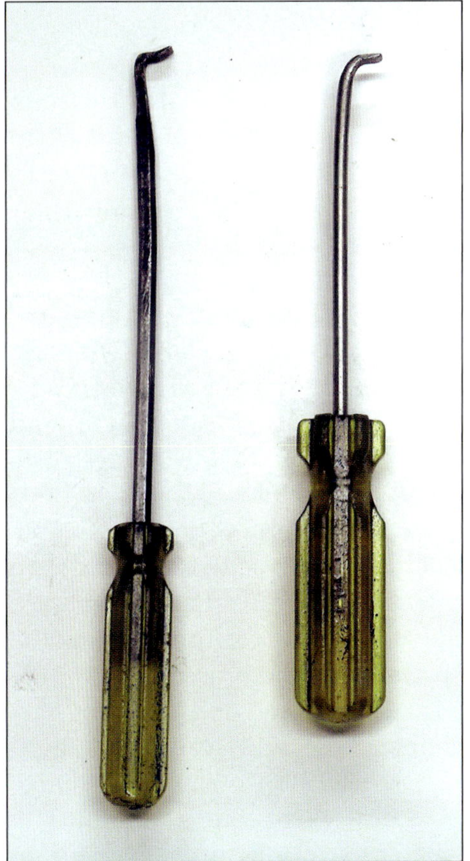

Here is the finished product—a couple of small screwdrivers, modified by heating then bending the ends over. They will come in handy for pulling steel and friction plates from the clutch drums.

REBUILDING

Rebuilding automatic transmissions has always been an area of the automotive hobby that has typically been left to professionals and a rare few hobbyists. I have known some extremely talented mechanics, and most still stay far away from any automatic transmission work. I've never fully understood why. Maybe it's the complexity of the valve body, or host of internal components, sprags, planetary gears, clutch packs, etc. At a glance it all certainly seems complicated. In reality, these transmissions can be correctly overhauled, and even upgraded, with a minimal amount of special tools and procedures.

Let's proceed and find out how simple these units can really be. A few special tools will be required here and there, but as outlined in Chapter 2, most can be found, purchased, or fabricated with a minimal amount of time and expense.

Transmission rebuilding requires a suitable work area. As the transmission is taken apart lay the parts out on a workbench. Pay close attention to the order in which they were removed from the case, and inspect each part for wear or damage.

The procedures described in this chapter apply to all years and models of the 700-R4, 4L60, and 4L60E units. Regardless of the year and model being worked on, the biggest difference between them will be in the valve-body area. The internal components remained basically the same through all years of production. Some minor improvements and upgrading occurred, but the basic relationship and arrangement of the

A transmission-holding fixture will prove invaluable. Some units allow the transmission to be rotated and locked in various positions.

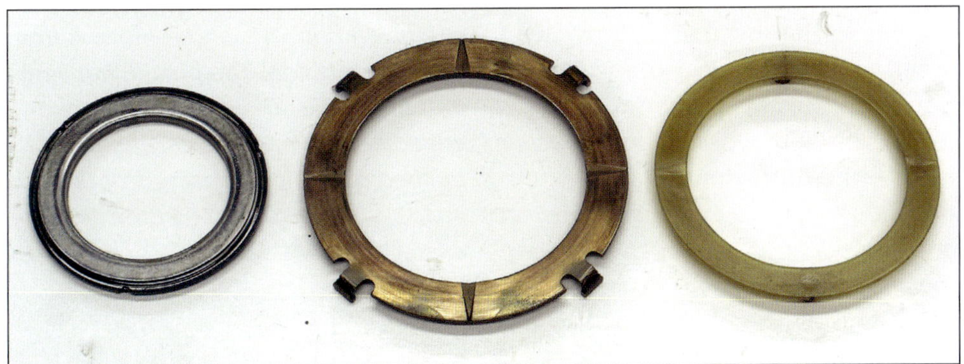

Transmissions use thrust washers between components to allow them to turn at different speeds without wearing out their mating surfaces. Some thrust washers are made of plastic (right), others are made of metal and may have a soft babbit or brass surface (center), others are the Torrington-bearing variety. Torrington bearings use tiny needle bearings between two metal halves (left).

internals remained the same, even for electronically controlled units.

One must keep in mind that when working with any year or model of the 700 transmission, you can remove all of the internal components down to the low/reverse apply piston without disturbing the valve body. The valve body can be left in place, and then carefully removed after removing the internals from the unit. You must pay very close attention to the valve body and the fasteners that attach it to the case, especially for the electronically controlled units, as several different length fasteners were used.

Once you have found a suitable work area, the transmission should be held in some sort of holding fixture. Having the unit at waist level or slightly higher, and being able to rotate it, will greatly improve the rebuilding experience.

While you are taking the unit apart, you must keep in mind that we are starting your overhaul procedure. If the unit has failed, you want to try to find out what failed and why it failed. The unit may have also been apart before, and there is no guarantee that it was correctly re-assembled. Careful attention must be paid to the location and arrangement of the internal components. There are several basic rules for all automatic transmissions. Thrust washers are used between any two components that will contact each other and rotate at different speeds. Some thrust washers are metal, some are plastic, and others are Torrington bearings. Typically, metal and plastic washers will have tabs or holes to retain them, if required. Torrington bearings will often only work correctly if installed in one direction. Incorrect installation could cause catastrophic transmission failure. Pay close attention to the location and orientation of any and all thrust washers during disassembly of the unit.

As you disassemble your transmission, you want to closely inspect each part, looking for obvious damage, wear, or complete failure. Inspect the sealing rings, bushings, thrust washers, and Torrington bearings. Also inspect the surfaces that they mate with, looking for any obvious signs of wear, scratching, pitting, etc. Take note of any burnt frictions and steels, cracked lining or burnt band material, damage to the drum where the band applies, and any other unusual damage to hard parts. Excessive friction between components often "blues" them considerably, but

Inspect clutch packs for worn linings, or damaged or worn steel plates. Clutch packs that have been slipping will often leave blue (or hot) spots on the steel plates.

they still may function or be within specification. The transmission builder is essentially trying to locate any possible failure points, as well as the orientation of the parts. It is always best to lay the parts out in the order that they were removed from the case. Like anything else, they must go back in the order they were removed; no need to mix/match components and complicate the overhaul process by trying to figure out where everything went, in addition to correctly overhauling the unit.

Transmission Disassembly

The first item to remove from the transmission is the governor cover and governor. Governors were used on all non-electronically controlled units. The cover may be somewhat stubborn to remove, especially if the vehicle the transmission came from was operated in a northern climate where they salt the roads heavily. It can be advantageous to apply some penetrating oil around the cover prior to removing it. A large flat-tip screwdriver and hammer work well for driving off the cover. A large round punch with the end ground at a slight angle also works well. Removing the governor prevents damage to the soft plastic drive gear; it will pull right out of the transmission once the cover is removed.

Remove the governor cover with a large flat-blade screwdriver or punch. It does not use a retainer, and is simply driven back into place with a new seal during the rebuilding process.

If you are working on a two-wheel-drive unit, remove the extension-housing bolts and the extension housing. Do not attempt to remove the speedometer gear or electronic speed-sensor assembly from the tail housing at this time.

The oil pan is removed next, to gain access to the TCC solenoid and the oil filter. This is also a good time to remove any wiring under the pan, and the connector that goes through the case, on the 4L60 models. The valve body will prevent removing the wiring harness on 4L60E models until it is removed, but it is still a good idea to unhook all the switches. The shift valve directly above the TCC solenoid must be removed on 4L60E models to facilitate its removal.

You are now ready to remove the pump bolts and the oil pump. GM did not provide threads to the outer

Unless the unit is from a 4WD application, it will have an extension housing and either speedometer gears or an electric speed sensor. Remove the four bolts, gently tap the extension housing, and remove it from the transmission. The plastic housing that holds the speedometer gears or speed sensor must be carefully pushed out of the housing from the inside. Use care here, as they are easily broken.

For the 4L60E models, removing the TCC solenoid requires removal of the shift solenoid valve just above it. The solenoid must be removed from the pump, before the pump can be pulled from the case.

The pump holes are not threaded for a slide hammer puller like most other GM transmissions. If the GM special tool isn't available, you can pry the pump out of the case with a large pry bar or screwdriver. A small amount of penetrating oil should be used around the pump housing to help loosen it up, especially if the vehicle was operated in a northern climate where the roads were salted in the winter.

pump housing, so a slide hammer can't be used to remove the pump. Once the bolts are removed, a large pry bar or screwdriver is required to push the pump out of the case.

Prior to removing the pump, you need to check the input-shaft endplay. If you have a dial indicator, record the endplay for reference. If not, pull the input shaft in and out to get an idea of how much play is present. Although it is best to have a dial indicator, it is not mandatory. We simply need to assure that the endplay is not excessive. It can be corrected during assembly with selective washers. The recommended endplay is .015 in to .036 in.

With the pump removed, locate the thrust washer. More often than not it will be sitting on the reverse drum. Place it back on the pump. Reach into the lower part of the case with a large flat screwdriver, and disengage the band from the retaining pin. The band can now be removed. It may be a bit stubborn, as the struts on the pin end must be worked up through the openings in the case, but it will come right out.

If a dial indicator is available, check main shaft endplay before taking the transmission apart. Selective washers are used to control endplay, and you may have to make adjustments upon final assembly. Endplay should be between .015 in and .036 in.

Reach in with a large flat blade screwdriver and disconnect the end of the band from the anchor pin. Using the same screwdriver, disengage the other end of the band from the case lugs as shown in the picture. This will then allow the band to be removed from the case.

Remove the reverse drum and input housing by grabbing the turbine shaft and pulling both assemblies out of the case. Lift the reverse drum off of the input housing, and note at this time the condition of the Teflon sealing rings on the turbine shaft. If your unit has scarf-cut Teflon seals, it is either an early unit, or they were installed during an earlier overhaul.

Remove the input sun gear. Using a pair of suitable snap-ring pliers, remove the snap ring that retains

Once the band is removed, you can grab the input shaft and remove the input and reverse drums as one assembly.

The input sun gear is removed next; it will lift right out of the front planetary gear assembly.

The output-shaft snap ring is removed next. A pair of snap-ring pliers is required, and you may need to support the output shaft, as it can fall out of the transmission when the snap ring is removed.

The early style overdrive sprag (right) used fewer elements and did not have a retainer. The larger and stronger OD sprag assembly on the left can be used in any earlier unit; just omit the thrust washer on the front planetary.

Early units will have two holes in the front planetary gear. If an early-style OD (overdrive) sprag is used, a thrust washer will be used on the front of the planetary gear. Later units, made in and after 1987, used an improved sprag design, and no thrust washer was required. The planetary gears are still interchangeable between years, and transmissions made in or after 1987 may still contain the holes for the thrust washer, even if it isn't used.

Once the snap ring has been removed from the front of the output shaft, you can remove the front planetary, carrier, sun shell, and sun gear. Note the location of both thrust and Torrington bearings between these components.

the forward planetary to the output shaft. Make sure to support the output shaft, as it may fall out of the transmission when the snap ring is removed. Lower the output shaft carefully from the transmission. It is okay to leave it in place, as it may be retained by adhesive from the factory if the unit has not been previously rebuilt. Some builders also stake it to the lower internal reaction gear so it will not fall out. It can be used to remove the forward planetary gear, reaction carrier, sun shell, and the sun gear. Note that there are thrust washers or Torrington bearings between these components, and one under the sun shell. On early units, the forward planetary will have a thrust washer and two retaining holes.

This thrust washer is not used with 1987-and-newer units, or any unit that has been retrofitted with the later-OD (overdrive) sprag assembly, even if the holes are present in the planetary. (Most thrust-washer kits will contain this thrust washer, even if it isn't used.)

Remove the front planetary, reaction carrier, sun shell, and sun gear, noting the location and orientation of the Torrington bearings and thrust washers between these components. The sun-shell thrust washer is black

The center support is held in position by a large snap ring. The snap ring is positioned so that one end keeps the retaining spring, oftentimes called an "anti-clunk" spring, in position in the case.

plastic, and will often stick to the bottom of the sun shell, instead of the inner race for the low roller clutch.

If still in place, remove the thrust washer that was under the sun shell, and the inner race for the low/reverse sprag. The race may need to be rotated while pulling it out, to release it from the sprag rollers. The center support is removed next. With a large flat-tip screwdriver, remove the large snap ring at the case lugs.

Note the retaining spring's location. It may be necessary to compress the retaining spring to remove the center support. Some center supports can be stubborn to remove, especially if the unit has experienced heavy case-lug wear. A scribe or screwdriver with a hooked end can be used to pull under the sprag to facilitate removal of the center support, while compressing the retaining spring at the same time.

Remove the lower planetary, and the low/reverse frictions and steels. Remove the reaction carrier under the planetary, which contains the

Removing Output Shaft and Reaction Carrier

With some units you will find it very difficult to remove the center support to gain access to the components under it. This occurs due to wear at the case lugs where they contact the center support. It is very difficult to compress the retaining springs and remove the center support at the same time, as it may be caught under the worn portion of the case lugs. With the output shaft still in place, grasp it and pull upward sharply. This will usually break the center support free from the case, and remove the output carrier, low planetary, low/reverse clutch pack, and the center support as a unit.

I have seen units worn to a point where I had to put a blanket or rags under the transmission, invert it in the holding fixture, and use a soft-faced mallet to drive the output shaft and associated internals from the case. If this becomes necessary, keep the output shaft pressed tightly down to avoid damage to the internal components while driving it out of the case. If you have an assistant available, they can put on a heavy-duty leather glove and grab the upper portion of the input shaft to assist removal from the case. Use caution here, as the inside of the case has very sharp edges.

Compressing the retaining spring and pulling it from the case with a hooked screwdriver or scribe can usually remove the center support. If the unit has considerable wear at the case lugs, the center support may not lift up and out of the case. An alternate method to remove the center support is to use the output shaft. A couple of soft blows to the output shaft are usually all that is needed to drive the center support from the case lugs.

If the output shaft is used to drive the center support from the case, it will also remove all of these components as well.

In order to facilitate removal of the low/reverse apply piston, you must remove the two bolts and the guide for the parking-pawl rod. This will allow the pawl to move back far enough so the apply piston can be blown out of the case with compressed air.

dogs (big square-cut teeth) that engage the parking pawl. Note that there is a Torrington bearing under the planetary; it will interchange with the Torrington bearing that is used under the front reaction carrier.

The last item to remove is the low/reverse apply piston from the case. It is necessary to remove the two bolts holding the guide assembly for the parking pawl so the parking pawl will move out of the way enough to remove the piston from the case.

Our homemade spring compressor will compress the spring cage far enough to remove the snap ring. Once the snap ring and spring cage are removed, you can remove the low/reverse apply piston.

A suitable tool is required to compress the spring cage over the apply piston to remove the snap ring. Once the snap ring is removed, apply compressed air to the case to remove the apply piston. This step will have to wait a few minutes until you have removed the valve body and separator plate.

Last on the list is to remove the servo assembly that applies the band. These can be extremely stubborn, as road salt may have the servo cover heavily corroded. Apply a good amount of penetrating oil prior to attempting removal of the servo assembly. Using a soft-faced hammer, tap the center of the cover several times. Push in on the cover and pry out the retaining ring. Pull the cover out to access the large blue O-ring. Grab the O-ring with a small pair of needle-nose pliers, or a scribe. Hold the ring, cut it, and pull it out of the cover. This will make removing the servo assembly much easier. Lay the entire assembly on the workbench and don't forget the return spring.

Compressed air can be applied to the low/reverse piston feed hole in the case once the valve body is removed. This is best accomplished with the transmission facing the floor, and a few rags, towels, or blankets under the unit to catch the piston and keep it from getting damaged.

You are now ready to remove the valve body and other items located under the transmission oil pan. Both electronic and non-electronically controlled units will have a wiring harness under the oil pan. For early 700s and 4L60s, there were several different arrangements used to apply the TCC solenoid.

This may have the wiring routed through a temperature switch, and one or more pressure switches. If not done already, remove the wiring from all connectors. The wiring harness is hard wired into the TCC solenoid, which was already removed from the oil pump prior to removing the transmission internals. For the 4L60E units, the electrical connectors may be difficult to remove without breaking the retainers. They become hard and brittle with use. Don't worry if one or all of them break—more than likely you will

The servo is retained in the case with a large ring. Apply some penetrating oil around the retaining ring to help loosen up the assembly. A couple of light blows with a soft-faced mallet will loosen up the servo cover, and facilitate removal of the retaining ring. A small screwdriver or awl can be used to get under one edge of the ring. It may help to push inward on the servo cover at the same time.

A neat trick to removing the servo assembly from the case is to cut the outer O-ring and pull it from its groove with a pair of needle-nose pliers. The servo assembly will then come right out of the case. Some transmissions will require a small amount of penetrating oil around the servo cover to help the process. Using a small flat-tip screwdriver, work the O-ring out of the groove. Cut it with a pocketknife or pair of wire cutters. Grab one end with a pair of needle-nose pliers and pull it out of the groove. The servo cover and assembly can be easily removed from the transmission.

need to install a new wiring harness anyhow.

Remove all of the components found under the oil pan. Remove the manual valve and parking-pawl rod first to facilitate easy removal of the valve body as the spool valve rod connects the linkage to the valve body. Remove the valve body, paying close attention on the 4L60E units as to the length of the bolts. On the 4L60 models, the TV cable is attached to the valve body. All models will

Removing the bolt over the leaf spring will take the spring pressure off the rooster comb. The leaf spring engages the rooster comb to provide detents for the different shift-selector positions.

have a leaf spring to engage with the manual valve's rooster comb to keep the transmission in the selected gear.

On auxiliary-valve-body 4L60s, the oil tube from the pump to the valve body will need to be removed prior to removing the valve body. It will help to mark the valve body to reference the oil tube's bolt/retainer. This simply eliminates confusion when putting the tube back in place.

4L60 units made in and after 1987 will have an auxiliary valve body and oil tube running to it from the oil pump. The oil tube is removed prior to removing the auxiliary or main valve bodies. Remove the bolts that hold the retainers for the tube, and gently pull the tube out of the pump and auxiliary valve body.

With all models, lift the valve body straight up with the transmission as level as possible. Once the valve body is removed, note the amount and location of any check balls. Even if they fall or roll off the separator plate, don't panic. The steel balls will have left wear marks or patterns on the plate, so you will still know how many were used, and their exact locations.

Steel Check Balls and Separator Plates

Steel check balls were used through the years of production. It is not uncommon to find wear patterns on the separator plate, and on occasion where the steel balls have worn holes in the plate so large that they are stuck in the plate, or have passed through to the other side. This requires replacing the separator plate, or installing an available aftermarket repair at the worn location. For minor wear, the steel plate can be peened with a machinist's hammer, and an old check ball used to provide a new sealing surface. This sort of repair should only be used for plates with minor wear; I highly recommend replacing excessively worn separator plates with new ones.

Seating the holes with an old steel check ball and a hammer can repair separator plates that have very minor wear. With the plate lying on a flat metal block, you can gently drive an old steel check ball into the plate to form a good seat.

Remove the auxiliary valve body (1987–1992 auxiliary VB models only), the 1-2 accumulator housing, and any other items on top of the separator plate. Note the location of the piston and the spring for the 1-2 accumulator housing. Some are installed with the piston facing the housing and the spring on the plate, while others will have the spring in the housing and the piston facing the plate. The arrangement of these parts may deviate from what the factory originally set them up with. Some shift kits or builders will disable the accumulators by leaving out the springs or reversing them, etc., to firm up shifts. The best course of

Remove the auxiliary valve body, noting that there is a check ball between it and the separator plate.

Three screws attach the 1-2 accumulator housing to the case. Note that they are different lengths and should be kept with the accumulator housing to avoid mixing them up with other valve-body bolts. Also note the orientation and location of the spring and the accumulator piston. Some units have the spring against the steel plate; others have the spring in the housing and the piston against the plate.

The separator plate goes between the transmission case and the valve body. Gaskets are used on each side of the plate. There were dozens of different plates used for various applications, and they should not be interchanged. If the plate is damaged beyond repair, obtain the exact replacement.

action is to return the unit to its original configuration. If installing a shift kit, follow the directions exactly for the unit you are working with.

Remove the separator plate. Look for any excess wear where the steel balls may have worn heavily on the separator plate. These holes will have to be repaired, or the plate will have to be replaced.

Remove any gaskets on the transmission that were under the plate. If possible, try to salvage the gaskets intact, so they can be matched up with the new gaskets from the rebuild kit. The gaskets will have a "C" for the case, and a "VB" for the valve body.

Important note It is also important to read any instructions or notes provided with your rebuild kit. Most kits cover several years of 4L60 transmissions and contain extra gaskets and other parts. They will note the changes made and the correct gaskets to use for the different years of transmissions.

You now need to locate, reference, and count the check balls used in the transmission case. This is an important part of the process, as there were several changes made to the case, and to the number of check balls used under the plate, for various years and models. There may be

Valve body and case gaskets on each side of the separator plate are marked for reference: "V" for the gasket against the valve body, and "C" for the gasket against the case. Several different gaskets were used, and the rebuild kit may contain several different ones. If possible, save the old gaskets intact, and always read any notes or updates supplied with the rebuild kit, or mentioned in any technical publications or service manuals.

On occasion you will find where a steel ball may have heavily worn the separator plate. Sometimes the ball will actually be stuck in the plate, or have passed clear through the plate. The separator plate will require repair or replacement.

TH-700-R4
(LATE KIT)

This kit only contains the late design V.B. gaskets (1987-on). These gaskets are not interchangeable with the early model and should not be used when servicing 1982-86 TH-700-R4 transmissions.

GOOD REBUILDING PROCEDURE DICTATES THAT GASKETS BE MATCHED PRIOR TO INSTALLATION.

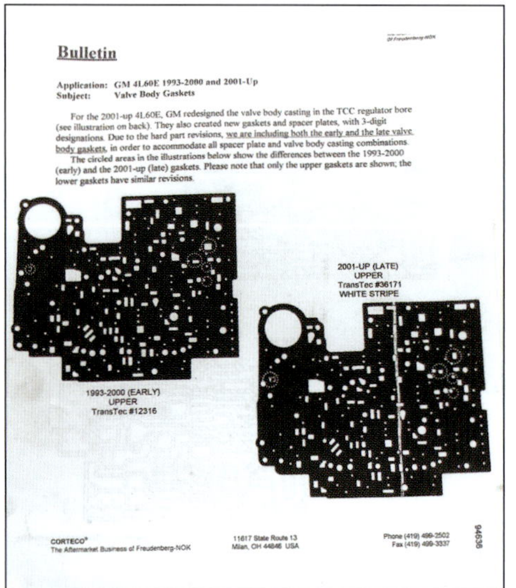

Bulletin

Application: GM 4L60E 1993-2000 and 2001-Up
Subject: Valve Body Gaskets

For the 2001-up 4L60E, GM redesigned the valve body casting in the TCC regulator bore (see illustration on back). They also created new gaskets and spacer plates, with 3-digit designations. Due to the hard part revisions, we are including both the early and the late valve body gaskets, in order to accommodate all spacer plate and valve body casting combinations.

The circled areas in the illustrations below show the differences between the 1993-2000 (early) and the 2001-up (late) gaskets. Please note that only the upper gaskets are shown; the lower gaskets have similar revisions.

1993-2000 (EARLY)
UPPER
TransTec #12316

2001-UP (LATE)
UPPER
TransTec #36171
WHITE STRIPE

CORTECO®
The Aftermarket Business of Freudenberg-NOK

11617 State Route 13
Milan, OH 44846 USA

Phone (419) 499-2502
Fax (419) 499-3337

94636

Pay close attention to any notes included with your rebuild kit. Companies that make rebuild kits may update information contained in their kits, based on manufacturers' service technical bulletins. Some rebuild kits also contain gaskets and other parts that help them cover a broader range of applications. Make sure to read all information included in the rebuild kit before rebuilding the transmission.

Check balls were used to provide one-way oil flow to various parts of the transmission. These steel check balls have passages in the case cast out for them. Not all of the check balls and passages were used for all models. In addition, some shift kits may have specific directions for installing case and valve-body check balls. Make sure to follow the directions exactly.

channels or places in the case that would accept a check ball, but they are not used for that year/model of transmission. To complicate this part of the rebuild, transmission fluid may be covering the check balls so you can't see them. Carefully tilt the unit enough to allow the fluid to drain away, but just enough so the check balls stay in place. Locate and remove the check balls, noting their original location. Again, if you get confused, the separator plate will have wear marks to identify their original locations and how many were used.

Some models will have a check ball located in a retainer or capsule near the lower portion of the pan. It may or may not come out. It should be left in place if the retainer will still hold it. It's pretty common for the staked portion to allow the check ball to fall out. I prefer to remove this check ball prior to cleaning the case

1987 and later 4L60 transmissions used one case-located check ball. It is pretty common for this check ball to fall out of its staked capsule. Make sure to install one in this location during rebuilding.

The anchor pin for the band is located in the case under the valve body. It can and will fall out of the case during cleaning. Make sure to remove it before taking the case out of the holding fixture for cleaning.

so it doesn't get lost. It can be put back in place and the tiny ears on the capsule staked to retain it during reassembly.

Remove the anchor pin for the band. This is commonly forgotten (and the pin lost) during cleaning. With all of the components removed, you should now be looking at a bare case ready for cleaning and inspection.

Heavy deposits on the outside of the case are best removed with a scraper and wire brush. Heavy-duty engine degreasers can really help loosen up heavy road dirt, oil, and

Being under the vehicle and behind the engine, the transmission gets it share of road dirt, oil, and grease. In northern climates where the roads are salted, the metal may be oxidized as well. Once your case is stripped down, a quick trip to a local car wash is a good way to remove most of the heavy deposits.

Once you have your case cleaned, it can be painted to protect the surface from oxidation and corrosion. Make sure to completely degrease the unit with brake cleaner. It also helps to warm it up slightly to help the paint penetrate the surface and dry quickly without runs.

grease. Undercoating and other hard deposits still require some scraping and manual cleaning. You want your case as clean as possible to avoid introducing any grit, grime, or other foreign materials into the assembly during overhaul. A quick trip to a local car wash is well worth the effort.

Once the case is cleaned and ready to assemble, it can be painted or clear coated to prevent oxidation. I use and prefer cast-finish paint, or stainless-steel paint, to duplicate the original finish. Just prior to painting the case, spray it down with brake cleaner or some other degreaser that dries without leaving a residue or oil coating. For a perfect job the case can be warmed right before painting it. I use an old two-burner gas stove, and heat the case for about 10 minutes. This helps dry the paint quickly and prevents runs.

If the case is going to be left unattended or there is a time lapse before assembly begins, obtain a large 55-gallon leaf bag, and bag the transmission to prevent the introduction of airborne dirt and debris. It is also important to bag the case between assembly sessions. Dirt and debris are the most common reasons that transmission rebuilds meet with less than acceptable results.

One of the most important parts of building a transmission is to keep dirt and debris out of the assembly. A large heavy-duty plastic bag should be placed over the transmission between building sessions. Also, cover any parts on the workbench that have been cleaned and are ready to build or install into the case.

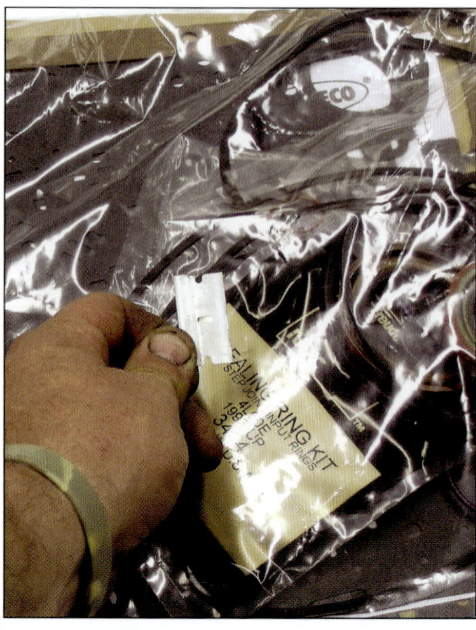

Be extremely careful when opening up the seal package. A knife or razor blade could cut and damage the lip seals.

Assembling the Transmission

Now that your case is cleaned and painted, you are ready to start assembly. Your transmission rebuild kit should be opened up, and the parts laid out for easy access. Use care when cutting the plastic that contains the seals, as the slightest cut to any of the lip seals can lead to devastating results.

The first item to inspect or replace is the bushing in the case. I

Lay out all of the parts from your rebuild kit for easy access during the rebuilding process. This is a good time to remove the frictions from the kit and soak them in clean ATF (automatic transmission fluid).

Bushings are relatively easy to remove. With your modified punch, simply catch the end of the bushing and drive it downward. If you can locate the factory parting line on the bushing, drive at this point. In most cases this will cause the bushing to separate and nearly fall out of its bore. Also make sure to inspect the bore before installing a new bushing to make sure you didn't scratch the surface and leave any high spots. Use fine-grit auto-body sandpaper to gently remove any high spots, if present, before installing the new bushing.

Once you have located a suitable driver for your new bushing, it should be driven into place. It is best to place the part on a large block or between blocks of wood, as needed, to facilitate driving in your new bushing without damaging the part.

Apply a small amount of red Loctite to your bushing prior to driving it into position. Also note that some bushings are driven in flush with the part surface, others may be driven into and stop on a shoulder, and others are driven below flush with the surface.

The low/reverse piston has a large square boss cast into its surface to keep it from turning in the case.

recommend removing and replacing all of the bushings and thrust washers in the transmission. There are several reasons for doing so. Any wear in the bushings and thrust washers, no matter how slight, allows for movement of the internals when the transmission is in operation. Excessive movement accounts for more gear noise, poor sealing at the rings, and increased wear to internal components—and in extreme cases, less than satisfactory transmission shift performance. By installing a full set of bushings, thrust washers, and the correct selective washer, you can set your new transmission up at minimal clearances. Having minimal up/down and fore/aft movements will reduce gear noise, improve transmission function, and increase longevity.

Most bushings are relatively easy to remove. Before driving one out, note its approximate position, depth below a flush surface, etc. You want to install your new bushing in the same position. Use some red Loctite to retain them, and use a suitable bushing driver to install the new bushings. In most cases, a driver can be fabricated from an old engine valve. This works fine for flush-mounted bushings, but some will need to be set below flush. A neat trick to set them below flush is to use an old bushing under the driver, if

Using a marker, place a line in the case and on the outer surface of the low/reverse apply piston to facilitate correct installation into the transmission.

you don't have the correct bushing installation tool.

Once you have installed your case bushing, you need to install the low/reverse apply piston spring cage and snap ring. Note the location of the square part of the piston, and the corresponding notch in the case.

Put a mark on the piston and case with a magic marker to keep them aligned as the piston is installed. Install new seals, use lots of ATF or assembly lube, and push the piston into place. It must be fully seated before installing the spring cage. The piston should push easily into position—do not force it in place or drive it in with a hammer and punch, or it will tear the seals. The piston can be pushed into place by hand; it helps to rock the piston a bit to get the seals down past the chamfered edges in the case, but it will push all the way down with a bit of effort. Make sure to use extreme caution here, as there are some very sharp edges inside the case. Test fit the low planetary reaction carrier; make sure to put the Torrington bearing under it for this procedure after submerging it in clean ATF. Gently polish the bearing surface with 600-grit auto-body sandpaper, or fine emery paper, to remove any scratches or high spots that will ride in your new bushing. Lubricate with ATF, TransGel, or petroleum jelly. The carrier should turn freely with minimal side play. If there are tight spots, they will show up as shiny areas on the new bushing. This happens from time to time—no need to panic; on occasion the bushing will not start exactly straight and will expand slightly at its parting line. Just sand the tight areas with 600-grit paper until the carrier turns freely without any binding or tight spots. Use this same procedure for all of the bushings that are installed during assembly. Test fit, sand for clearance as needed, and lubricate for assembly.

Make sure to install the Torrington bearing under the carrier. The Torrington bearing should not be cleaned with solvents, other than submerging it in fresh ATF. If it has any rough or tight spots, replace the bearing. Install the correct Torrington bearing under the low/reverse planetary gear, and install the planetary.

Be sure to inspect the pinions—any tight or rough spots, or excessive endplay will require replacement. It should turn smoothly in the carrier

Install the low/reverse reaction carrier into the case first. Make sure to install a new case bushing. The Torrington bearing should be submerged in clean ATF, and then retained to the bottom of the carrier with a small amount of TransGel or petroleum jelly. Note: The carrier-to-case Torrington bearing will interchange with the Torrington bearing used under the front planetary carrier.

Check the pinions on the low/reverse planetary prior to installation. They should turn freely without any roughness or tight spots, and not show excessive endplay. The acceptable endplay for the pinions is .008 to .024 in. However, the play on all pinions should be very close to the same measurement. If any show quite a bit more endplay than others, the unit should be replaced.

without binding. The accepted endplay for planetary pinions is .008 to .0024 in. Later low/reverse planetary units will have an oil slinger. This was added around 1987. These later units can be used in all years, when replacement is required. Install the low planetary into the reaction carrier; make sure to install the Torrington bearing between the two parts.

You can now install your low/reverse frictions and steel plates. There were several different arrangements used through the years of production. The factory may have installed selective steels under the clutch pack. If used, install any waved or selective steels first, then start with a new steel plate, friction plate, and continue until you have installed five steels and five frictions, ending with a friction. The last friction rides against the underside of the center support. Make sure to check this surface for wear, especially if the removed low/reverse clutches were worn, burnt, or damaged. All friction material should be soaked in clean ATF for at least 15 minutes prior to installation into the transmission.

Technical note If the apply piston and/or center support requires replacement, it should be matched up exactly with the parts being replaced. The factory service manual and most technical manuals list the various pistons and center supports used through the years of production, and the addition and use of selective apply plates and waved apply plates, if used.

Make sure to soak all frictions in clean ATF for at least 15 minutes prior to installing them. A small plastic bucket, or 1.5-gallon ice-cream container, works well for this purpose. Your container of clean ATF can also be used to submerge Torrington bearings and planetary-gear assemblies right before putting them into the transmission. If you are going to work on something else while the frictions are soaking, you can also put the lid on the container to keep airborne dirt and debris out of the ATF.

An oil slinger was added to the low/reverse planetary in later-model transmissions. These later units will interchange into earlier units and vice versa. I have never seen that the oil slinger has helped reduce wear at the pinions. It's quite common to see excessive pinion play on either style when they are removed from high-mileage units.

4L60s used a waved apply plate combined with a selective plate for the low/reverse clutch pack. It is best to duplicate what was removed from the transmission during rebuilding.

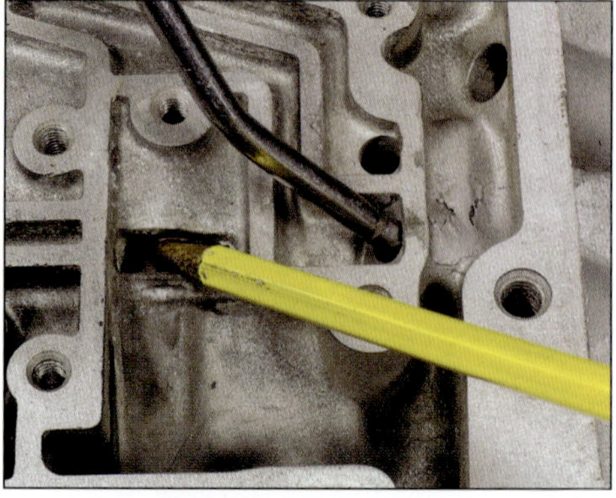

It is difficult to measure the low/reverse clutch-pack clearance, as the associated parts are enclosed in the transmission case. You can, however, apply some compressed air to the case, and observe the movement of the low/reverse apply piston. The low/reverse clutch is not involved with a shift, but it does need some clearance.

Mixing and matching of these components is not recommended, but sometimes the builder must custom stack the low/reverse clutch pack as one or more of the original items may have been altered previously, or replaced with an incorrect part. The bottom line is that the low/reverse clutch pack must have some clearance to work correctly. Since the clutch pack is not involved in a shift, having a lot of clearance will not affect the performance of the unit, other than possibly a very slight delay in engagement. It is perfectly acceptable to combine several steel plates (even used ones) against the low/reverse piston to reduce the clutch endplay clearance. Several old steel plates can also be combined to make up the approximate thickness of a waved plate and selective apply plate, if they are not being used. Consider .010 to about .035 in a good range to end up with. Apply air to the transmission case, and observe the movement of the apply piston once the transmission is assembled with the center support and snap ring in place.

Always install new steels and friction plates. Avoid using relined material, and insist on the very best. The OEM (Original Equipment

Early 4L60s used a weaker roller clutch or sprag assembly in the center support. The later design on the right was introduced in 1987, and is highly recommended for all rebuilds.

The center support is installed into the case and retained with a spring. The large snap rings are installed over the center support. Make sure one end of the snap ring ends up over the left edge of the retaining spring to keep it in place. When installing the center support, use a small amount of grease to hold the retaining spring in position in the case while the center support is pushed into position.

The low-sprag inner race must be turned clockwise while installing it into the low sprag. Make sure it is fully engaged with the front of the planetary gear. While turning the race clockwise, push down until it engages the front planetary—it will push easily into place and bottom out. There is no thrust washer under the race. A plastic thrust washer is used on the top of the race against the sun shell. Resist the urge to install a metal thrust washer at this location. TH350s used a metal thrust washer; 4L60s use a plastic washer.

Manufacturer) type friction materials are fine, although several companies will market "high-performance" friction materials. Nicely sanded, used steel plates will not deliver acceptable performance. Always replace them no matter how good they look.

You are now ready to install the center support. Replacing the low sprag is recommended, as the springs can weaken with age and start to come apart. Units made prior to 1987 will use a sprag with shorter rollers, and not as much holding capacity. The 1987-and-later roller sprag center support assembly is preferred, and is a direct replacement for the early style. The aftermarket also markets a bolt-in center-support assembly. This is highly recommended for high-performance applications.

Locate and install the center-support retaining spring—a dab of TransGel will hold it in place. Install the center support, snapping it into place over the retaining spring. Make sure it is fully seated, exposing the groove for the snap ring. Start the snap ring so that the leading edge of the ring is over the flat end of the retaining spring. Working in a clockwise direction, snap the ring into place, and gently seat it with a flat screwdriver and hammer.

Install the inner sprag race while turning it clockwise and pushing down at the same time. Install a new thrust washer on the race, retain with TransGel. Remove and replace the sun-gear bushings, install the sun gear, and then install the sun shell. Install a new thrust washer on the sun shell using TransGel and ensuring the four tangs are fully inserted into the corresponding holes in the sun shell. Install the upper planetary

The sun gear gets a new bushing. Note that it is set below flush and will require the correct driver to set its position below the surface.

A large, four-tang metal thrust washer is used between the front of the sun shell and the front carrier. Use a small amount of TransGel to retain the washer to the sun shell.

The output shaft is installed from the bottom. Work it up through the transmission until it protrudes far enough above the planetary to expose the groove for the snap ring. A small bottle jack can be used to hold the output shaft in place if you are working alone. Most rebuild kits come with a new snap ring for this location. Make sure it is fully seated in the groove. Pull sharply on the output shaft after the snap ring is installed to make sure it will not pop the ring off the shaft and allow the shaft to fall out.

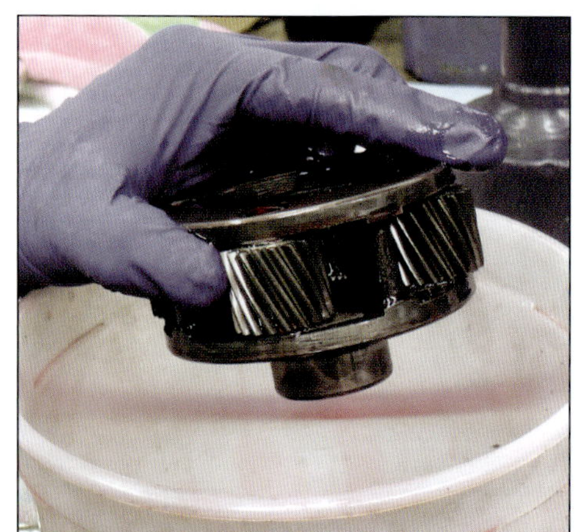

Submerge the planetary gear assembly in clean ATF prior to installing it into the case.

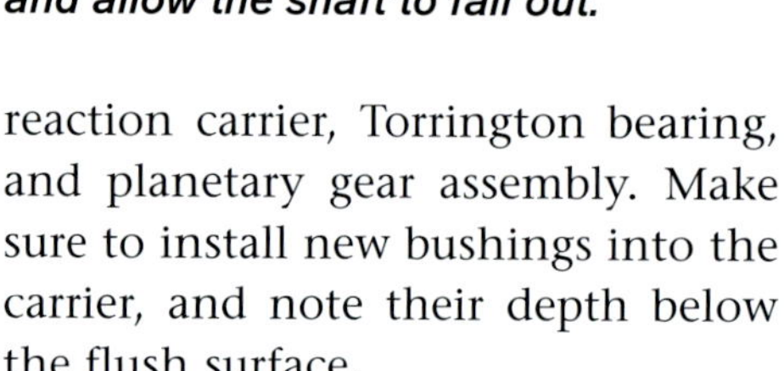

reaction carrier, Torrington bearing, and planetary gear assembly. Make sure to install new bushings into the carrier, and note their depth below the flush surface.

The output shaft is installed next, working it up from the bottom of the case. It helps to rotate the shaft during installation. While holding it up, install the snap ring. A small bottle jack can be used to hold the output shaft in place. Install the input sun gear over the upper planetary, large end down. If using an early-style overdrive sprag, install the thrust washer on the planetary. Using the two holes in the unit for the pins on the thrust washer, retain it with TransGel. Note: The later and stronger overdrive sprag is a direct replacement for the early-style sprags, and is highly recommended. If using the later sprag assembly, omit the thrust washer on the front planetary.

You are now ready to rebuild the input housing containing the forward, overrunning, and 3-4 clutch packs. This is the most important part of the assembly, and the most difficult. Using soft jaws, gently clamp the turbine shaft in a large vise with the drum end up. A hole can also be drilled in a large workbench to hold the unit during this procedure.

It is also important to note here that input drums were changed several times during the years of production, and not all of the internal components will interchange. Factory service publications, and most aftermarket technical publications, will outline the changes made, and interchange between parts, if applicable.

For the purpose of this publication, I recommend re-using the original components or matching them up exactly with any replacement components. The input drums also went through several design changes, most specifically between 1986 and 1987, and for both the 245-mm and 298-mm torque converters.

Remove the 3-4 clutch pack snap ring, then the 3-4 steels and frictions. The unit may use cushion springs (also called load-release

Gently clamp the turbine shaft in a soft-jawed vise. A couple of small boards or pieces of leather can be used to protect the shaft surface from the vise jaws.

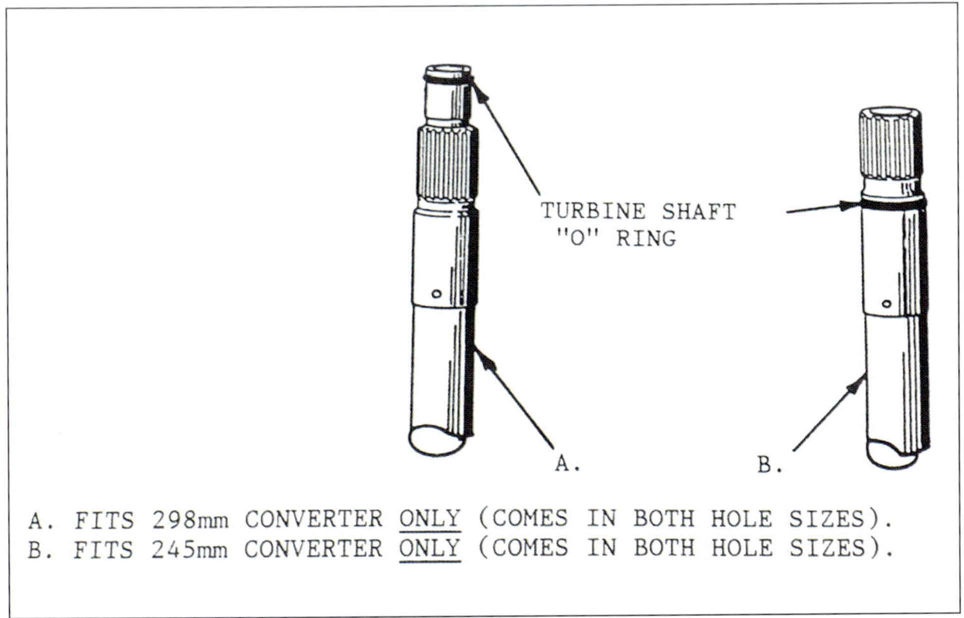

This picture from the ATSG (Automatic Transmission Service Group) service manual shows 298-mm and 244-mm turbine shafts and the feed-hole difference between different drums. If your input drum requires replacement, you must use a unit with the same casting number, feed-hole size, and input-shaft O-ring location.

The factory used load-release springs in some 3-4 clutch-pack assemblies. Most builders do not install them. Leaving them out provides quicker application of the 3-4 clutch pack, and improved shift "feel." You simply need to make sure that your separator plate has a hole at position #44 as shown. Use a 5⁄64-in drill bit to drill the hole, using the valve-body gasket as a guide.

With the drum securely held in a soft-jawed vise, carefully remove the large snap ring that retains the 3-4 clutch pack. Use care not to pry upwards on the snap rings, as it is possible to break the thin aluminum material off above the ring.

springs); they are not needed, as most builders do not install them.

Remove the large snap ring. This will facilitate the removal of the forward clutch pack, overdrive sprag assembly, forward apply piston, overrunning apply piston, and the overrunning clutch pack. The 3-4 apply spacer and the 3-4 apply piston can also be removed.

Using a large screwdriver or small pry bar, remove the snap ring over the forward backing plate. This is a very heavy-duty snap ring, and will require considerable effort to remove it from the drum.

3-4 Clutch Arrangements

There were several different 3-4 clutch-pack arrangements used through the years of production. The factory continued to upgrade the design using more frictions, thicker steels, and thicker solid apply plates. The later setups will be the best, using one thick steel apply plate, and the thick frictions and steels. In order to retrofit the later setups into earlier units, you must have all the components that apply the clutch pack from the drum, as the arms on the apply ring between the 3-4 apply piston and the apply plate will be different lengths.

The aftermarket also stepped up with high-capacity clutch-pack assemblies, which will work for all years. They provide enough components to successfully stack additional frictions, and increased holding capacity, into any year transmission. If used, follow the directions closely, as different components are required for different year transmissions. When replacing the factory configuration with anything else, simply try to use the shortest apply ring, the thickest apply plate, the most frictions and steel plates, and still end up with the correct clutch-pack clearance. The 3-4 clutch pack should have about .060 to .080 in endplay.

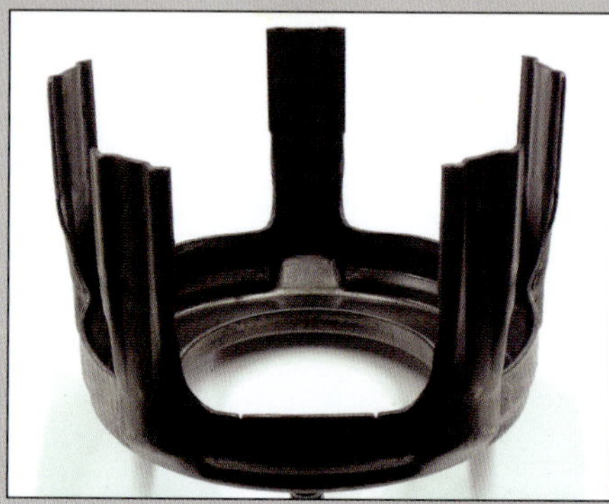

The 3-4 clutch pack uses an apply ring that sits on top of the apply spacer. Shown is a later setup used in a 4L60E unit. The later setups are preferred, as they use a thick apply plate, short apply spacer, thick backing plate, thick steel plates, and six 3-4 clutch pack frictions.

Take time to note the arrangement of the direct and forward clutch packs. There were several different arrangements used, along with different thickness friction plates. A waved apply plate is used with the forward clutch pack.

Input Drum Rebuilding

The input drum is connected directly to the turbine shaft. It contains the forward clutch assembly, overrunning clutch assembly, 3-4 clutch assembly, and the overdrive sprag clutch. The factory made several changes to the design to improve durability and transmission performance. Most important was the introduction and use of a stronger 28-element overdrive-sprag assembly. All units made in and after 1987 will have the stronger sprag clutch. The stronger sprag clutch can be installed into any year transmission by simply installing the clutch and

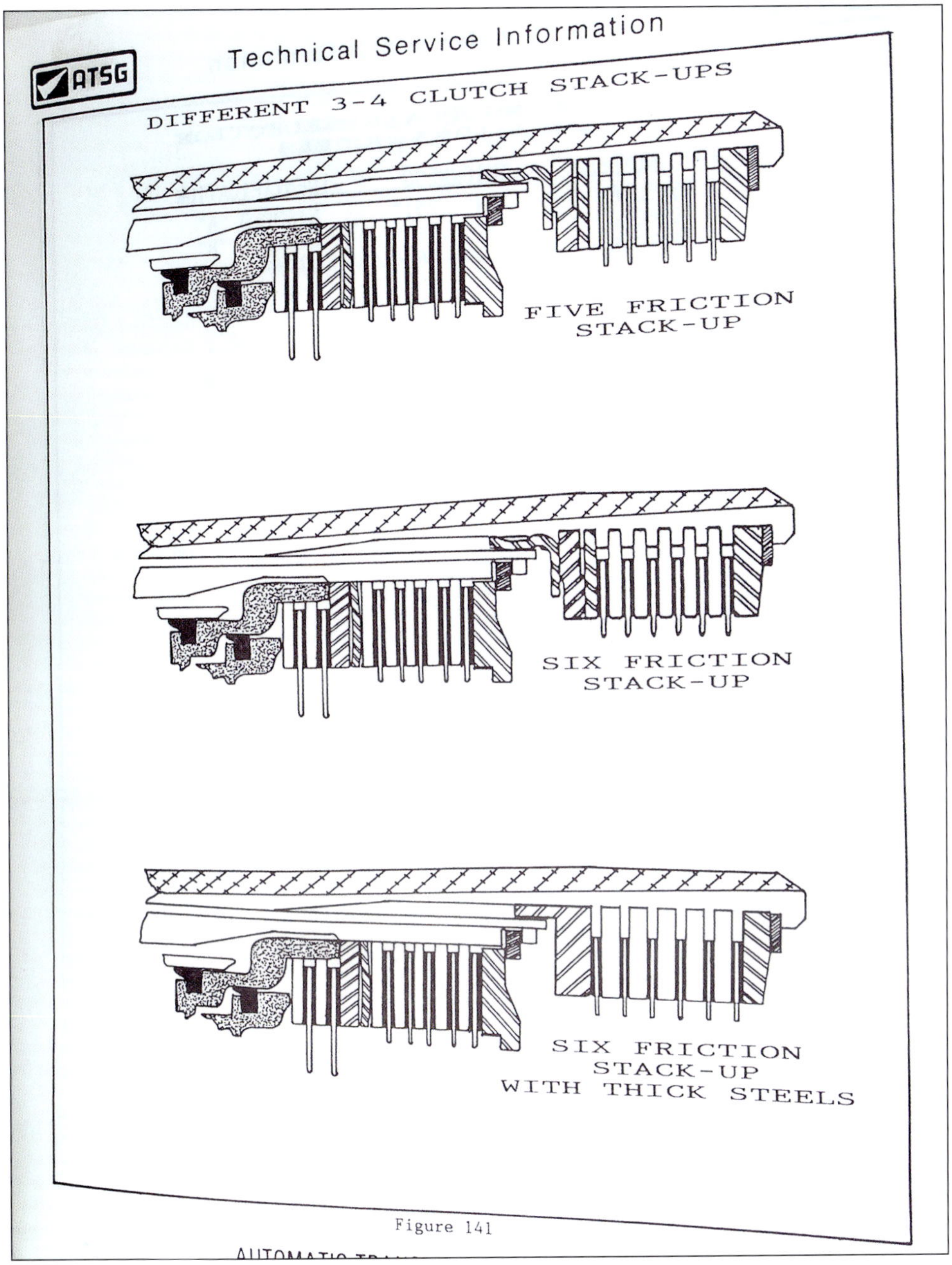

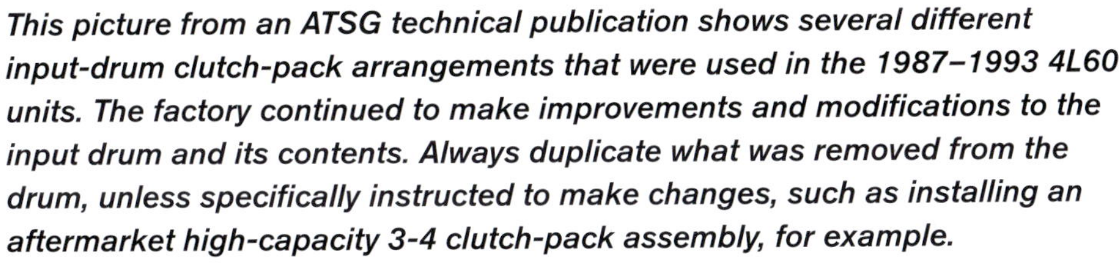

This picture from an ATSG technical publication shows several different input-drum clutch-pack arrangements that were used in the 1987–1993 4L60 units. The factory continued to make improvements and modifications to the input drum and its contents. Always duplicate what was removed from the drum, unless specifically instructed to make changes, such as installing an aftermarket high-capacity 3-4 clutch-pack assembly, for example.

omitting the thrust washer on the front planetary gear. Other improvements included using a thick solid apply plate for the 3-4 clutch pack, and thicker steels and frictions. Molded apply pistons were also used for the 3-4, direct, and overrunning clutches. The molded 3-4 apply piston can be used in any input drum, and is highly recommended. In order

The factory upgraded the overdrive-sprag assembly to a 28-element unit. Here we have removed the snap ring and inner race. This improved holding power and durability of the sprag assembly. Early overdrive sprags used 26 elements, and required a thrust washer to be installed on the two holes on the front planetary-gear assembly.

The factory made numerous changes to the 3-4 clutch-pack assembly. This is a critical area of the transmission. The latest units used a thick solid apply plate, with six thick steels and frictions. The aftermarket offers thin, high-capacity 3-4 clutch packs, which come with selective apply plates to give the builder options when setting up the 3-4 clutch pack. The latest factory setup, as shown in the picture, is a very good design. It can be incorporated into any early drum; provided the correct height apply spacer is used.

The molded 3-4 apply piston is highly recommended for all rebuilds. The piston is made of steel, with the seals molded to it. This design is much stronger and eliminates two potential leak paths for the pressurized transmission fluid on the inner portion of the seals, as compared to the stock aluminum apply piston. The seal lips are also much stronger, more heat resistant, and less prone to failure compared to the stock lip seals. They are also much easier to install into the drum. Apply a liberal amount of clean ATF, and install the piston into the housing. No special tools are required for installing molded apply pistons, they will just about fall into place.

All of your components should be cleaned and inspected prior to assembling the input drum. Lip seals will need to be installed on all apply pistons, unless you have upgraded to the later-style molded apply pistons. Notice that the overrunning clutch apply piston has matching posts for each spring in the spring cage. If upgrading to a molded apply piston, you must also upgrade the spring cage to the later-style cage with integrated spring retainer.

to upgrade to the molded overrunning and forward clutch pack molded apply pistons, the spring case over the overrunning piston must be replaced with the later design.

Once the input drum assembly is cleaned and ready for assembly, gently clamp the turbine shaft in a shop vise. Use soft vise jaws if available, and clamp below where the sealing rings are located. Lubricate and install the O-ring into the bottom of the drum first. It is usually, but not always, green in color. In any case, as with all seals and O-rings, match it up carefully with the one removed from the drum. Lubricate and install the 3-4 apply piston. The aluminum piston may require the use of your seal-installing tool around the outer lip seal. The molded 3-4 apply piston will install easily by simply twisting it as you push it into the drum. Install the 3-4 apply spacer next, followed by the spring cage. Install the spring cage into the drum.

The next step is the most difficult. Install seals onto the overrunning and forward apply pistons, unless molded pistons are being used. Install the forward apply piston into the steel housing. Use the lip-seal installation tool if needed. The molded pistons usually go in by simply twisting them while applying slight downward pressure. Use plenty of petroleum jelly or TransGel

Continued on page 48

The first item installed into your drum is the O-ring. It provides the inner seal surface for the spacer that holds the forward and overrunning clutch apply pistons. In many kits, the O-ring will be green in color. Make sure to match it up exactly with the O-ring removed from the drum, and apply a generous amount of ATF or TransGel to the O-ring after it is in position.

The molded 3-4 apply piston is installed into the bottom of the input drum. Use plenty of lubricant, and twist the piston while pushing downward. In most cases it will fall into position with little effort. If you are using an aluminum apply piston with lip seals, you may have to use a lip-seal installation tool to get them started. The factory was generous enough to provide a wide chamfered area for the outer seal to make the piston relatively easy to install.

The 3-4 clutch apply spacer rests directly on top of the 3-4 apply piston. The long arms should be correctly oriented with the slots provided in the input housing. It should fall easily into place, and sits directly on the apply piston.

The spring cage is installed on top of the apply spacer. No lubricant or TransGel is needed, as the spring cage will self center on top of the apply spacer.

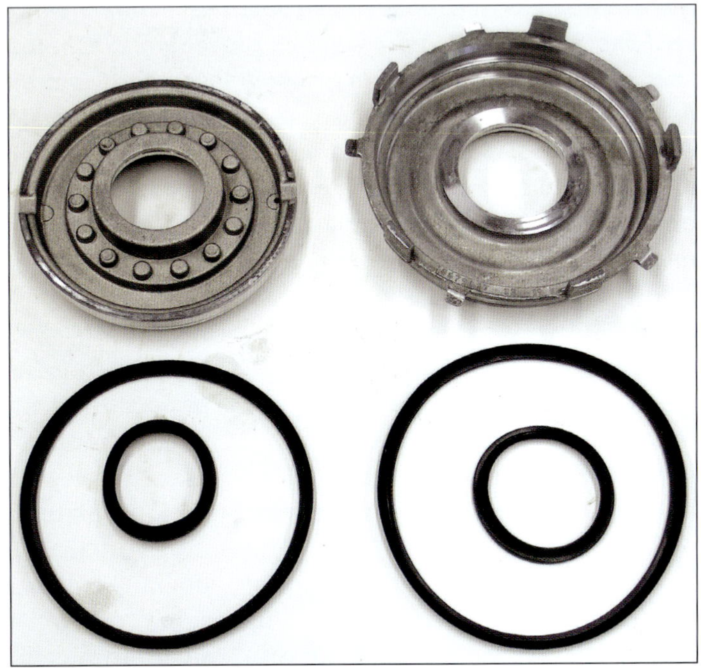

If you are using aluminum forward and overrunning apply pistons, locate the correct lip seals and install them on the pistons. The lips on all seals face down.

To facilitate the installation of the forward apply piston, it must be put inside of the steel housing before installing them into the drum. Using a liberal amount of TransGel on the outer seal, install the forward piston into the steel housing. Align the tangs on the forward piston with the correct slots in the input drum. Turn the drum on its side and install both parts into the input housing as one unit. The inner seal on the forward piston may need some help with your seal installation tool to get it past the snap ring groove in the center of the drum. Once past the groove, push down firmly on the assembly to seat it against the 3-4 apply spacer return spring. Install the overrunning apply piston into the forward apply piston, again using your seal installation tool to get the inner seal past the snap ring groove. This procedure eliminates the need to buy special seal installation tools to install these parts into the input drum. The key here is to use plenty of TransGel to hold the forward piston into the housing while being installed into the drum. Turning the drum on its side will help prevent the piston from falling out of the housing during installation. Once both pistons are in place and fully seated, install the spring cage and snap ring using a spring compressor.

There are tangs on the forward clutch piston that align with slots in the input drum assembly, as shown. They will end up just inside the long arms on the 3-4 apply spacer.

The tangs on the overrunning apply piston should align as shown, on either of the slots located between the deeper slots for the forward piston.

here. Both components will be installed together into the drum. Once fully seated, you can install the oversprung clutch apply piston, spring cage, clamp the unit back in the vise, compress the spring cage, and install the snap ring.

Install the seal for the output shaft at this time. Once the snap ring is fully seated, identify the overrunning steel and friction plates. Install a steel plate first, then friction, steel, and end with a friction plate. Install the thick backing plate that separates the overrunning and forward clutch packs.It is critical at this point to make sure that you have some clearance between the bottom of the backing plate and the first overrunning friction plate. The factory upgraded this area of the transmission, and two different friction and steel arrangements were used for both the overrunning and forward clutch packs. These components will not interchange.

Install the forward clutch pack into the drum, starting with a waved apply plate, then flat steel, friction, steel friction, and ending with a friction plate. The backing plate and retaining ring are not installed at this time. However, the backing plate should be installed temporarily, to make sure that you have sufficient forward clutch-pack clearance.

Continued on page 51

A single spring cage is used on top of the overrunning clutch piston. The spring cage will return either the forward or overrunning clutch pistons when the transmission is in operation.

A spring compressor is required to compress the spring cage far enough to install the snap ring.

The snap ring used here is a heavy-duty part, and requires a good pair of snap-ring pliers to facilitate its installation. Attempting to install or remove this ring with screwdrivers or other tools may spread and weaken the ring.

The seal in the end of the input drum seals off the fluid path to the output shaft.

Overrunning and forward steel plates are noticeably different. The steels on the right are for the overrunning clutch pack. Additional notches are provided on the forward steel plates. This prevents confusion and will not allow the forward steel plates to be installed in the lower part of the drum for the overrunning clutch pack.

All models and years of the 4L60 use two flat steel plates and two frictions for the overrunning clutch. Even so, early units used thinner frictions in this location. Make sure you have the correct frictions and steels for your transmission.

The correct installation of the overrunning clutch steels and frictions is shown here. The last friction plate should be just below the tip of the forward apply-piston tang.

Two important items are shown in this picture. Notice the gap between the backing plate and the last overrunning clutch friction. The first steel plate installed on the backing plate for the forward clutch pack is a waved plate. Some units used a flat steel plate after the waved plate. Some early units may use a waved plate directly against the first forward friction plate.

Clutch Packs

It is important to note here that the factory used several different arrangements for the forward clutch pack. The thick backing plate between the overrunning and forward clutch packs may vary in thickness between some units. Some units also used a waved apply plate directly on a friction, instead of pushing directly on a steel plate first. It is always best to attempt to duplicate what was removed from the transmission, while ensuring that both clutch packs have sufficient end clearance. There may be cases where someone has previously rebuilt the transmission and may have altered the arrangement of these components. In any and all cases, you must make the effort to ensure that your transmission is correctly assembled in this area, even if this means replacing all the components, from the apply pistons up, with known components from a good working unit, or buying all the associated items new from a parts supplier. It is highly recommended at this point to upgrade to the very latest apply-piston and clutch-pack arrangements, using molded pistons, the late-style spring cage, the thick steels and frictions, and thick solid apply plates.

The above photo is the later forward clutch pack. It consists of five flat steel plates and five flat friction plates. They stack directly onto a waved plate that rests on top of the thick apply plate. The waved plate is always installed first in all models, followed by the rest of the clutch pack. For the drum shown in the right photo, you are installing a flat steel plate, then alternating friction and steel plates, and ending up with a friction plate.

When upgrading to molded forward and overrunning apply pistons, you must use the later-style spring cage as shown. The early spring cage does not have a retainer for the bottom of the springs, only for the top.

Lubricate and install the Torrington bearing that goes between the input drum and the overdrive sprag. Install the overdrive sprag into the input drum, turning it in a clockwise direction to engage the forward and overrunning clutch friction plates. Work the sprag into the drum until it rests against the Torrington bearing. Install the forward clutch backing plate and snap ring.

The 3-4 clutch pack is installed next. The apply plate goes in first. The arms on the apply plate locate over the arms on the 3-4 apply

Continued on page 55

Overdrive Sprag Assembly

The overdrive sprag should be taken apart for cleaning and inspection. Prior to taking the sprag apart, check it for correct operation. By firmly holding the outer hub, the inner hub should turn clockwise but lock when attempting to turn it counterclockwise.

The overdrive sprag assembly is a one-way clutch. It should hold in one direction, and turn freely in the other. Make sure that the outer section turns clockwise when the center is held firmly, and vice versa. This check only tells you that the sprag is assembled correctly and holding. It will not tell you if the unit is damaged. It should be completely disassembled, cleaned, and inspected, and the sprag assembly replaced, if needed.

It should turn smoothly without binding or having tight or rough spots. Even if it turns freely, and locks in one direction, it does *not* mean that the unit is in good condition. The sprag should still be taken apart for visual inspection of the components. I have seen sprags that

In order to disassemble the overdrive sprag assembly, gently pry the inner snap ring out of its groove. Lift the inner hub off of the assembly. By turning the inner race clockwise, it will slide out of the sprag to facilitate removing the sprag from the outer race.

still functioned correctly, but when taken apart, the spring cage that holds the sprag elements was completely destroyed. Many units may also show considerable wear to the outer race. Remove the snap ring and spin the inner hub out of the sprag clutch.

Remove the upper and lower races from the sprag. Inspect all parts for wear. The "dogs" in the sprag assembly are held in place by a cage. Closely inspect the cage for damage, and inspect the sprag elements themselves for obvious wear, cracking, etc.

Reassemble the unit by installing the sprag clutch into the outer hub first, then the outer race, inner race, inner hub, and snap ring. Test the unit again; it must rotate clockwise, and hold when attempting to turn it counterclockwise.

Once the unit is completely disassembled, inspect all the components. Check the cage holding the sprag elements closely for cracked or broken sections. Also check the inner and outer races for wear. The sprag shown in this picture is the later-style sprag assembly with a built-in retainer. It is stronger than the early design, and will replace the early sprag without transmission modifications. Simply leave off the thrust washer that is used on the top of the front planetary during assembly of the transmission.

Install a new seal inside the input drum and place the Torrington bearing in position as shown. Make sure to submerge the bearing in clean ATF. Turn the inner section while holding the outer section stationary, to check for any roughness or tight spots. Replace the Torrington bearing if any damage is detected.

The overdrive sprag assembly must be fully seated against the Torrington bearing as shown. Turn the sprag clockwise to help engage it with the forward and overrunning clutches.

Once the overdrive sprag is fully seated against the Torrington bearing, install the forward clutch backing plate and snap ring. Make sure that the snap-ring ends are oriented between the lugs as shown, and that the ring is fully seated into the groove in the housing.

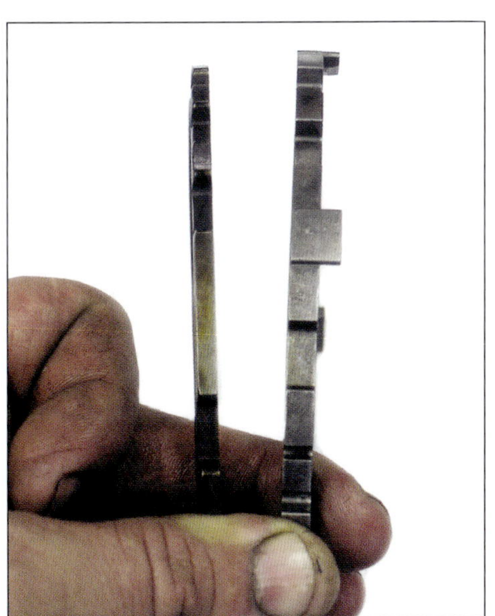

The late style 3-4 clutch pack is shown here. This is the most desirable setup for the 4L60 transmissions. The factory used several different arrangements over the years of production, and settled on using a solid apply plate with six thick steels and friction plates. Most early transmissions did not use this arrangement. Instead, they used a thin metal spacer on top of the apply-spacer ring, followed by at least one thick plate. The clutch pack would start out with a steel plate, then alternate friction, steel, friction, steel, and end up with the backing plate. These early 3-4 clutch packs work fine, but lacked the integrity of the later arrangement. The aftermarket offers high-capacity 3-4 clutch packs, with selective apply plates, to upgrade any year or model of 4L60 transmission.

The late style 3-4 apply plate is shown here, noting the arms that rest on the 3-4 apply spacer. The plate is installed with the arms down and into the large cutouts in the drum. It sits directly on the apply spacer. Once in place, the rest of the 3-4 clutch pack is installed, starting with a friction and alternating steel, friction, steel, friction, and ending with the thick steel backing plate.

Once the 3-4 clutch pack and backing plate have been installed into the drum, install the snap ring as shown, with the ends meeting between the lugs in the drum.

Once the 3-4 clutch-pack snap rings are installed in the drum, check the 3-4 clutch-pack clearance. The factory recommends .060- to .080-in clearance. With some high-capacity aftermarket 3-4 clutch packs, selective apply plates are provided so the builder can adjust clearance as required. The aftermarket kits also contain thin steels and frictions, which can be used in conjunction with stock parts, if you are building the drum from scratch, or do not have all of the correct factory components available. In any case, it is recommended to apply the 3-4 clutch pack several times by using compressed air to the hole in the turbine shaft between the sealing rings. This will seat the components and provide a more accurate measurement of the clutch-pack endplay.

Once the input drum is fully assembled, air check the clutch packs by applying compressed air as shown. Listen carefully for leakage inside the drum as the pistons apply the clutch packs.

Install the selective washer over the turbine shaft. Reuse the original washer for initial endplay checks.

Install the Torrington bearing as shown on top of the selective washer. Make sure it has been submerged in clean ATF, and check for binding or rough spots; replace the bearing if any problems are detected.

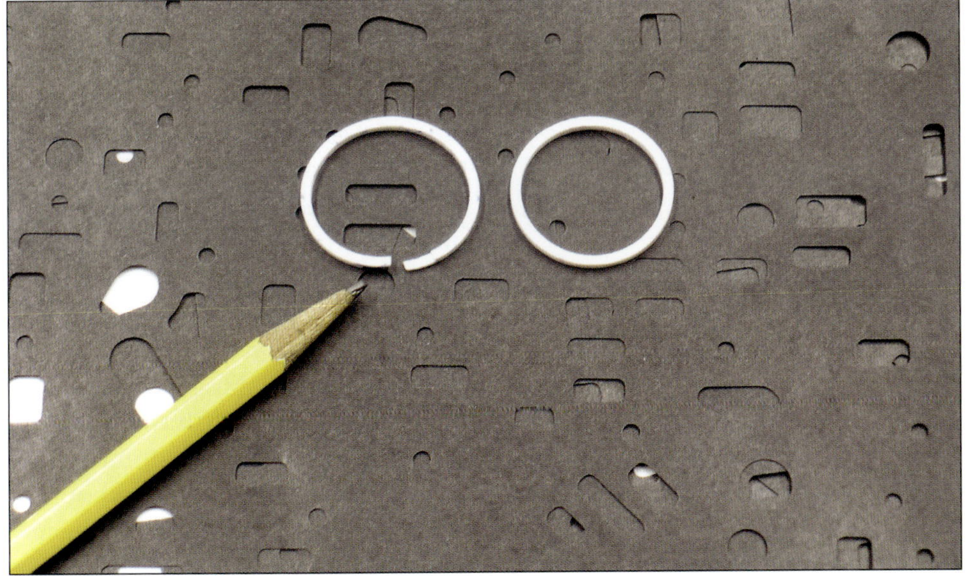

Some kits will include cut rings as well as solid Teflon rings. Resist the urge to use the cut rings, they will not seal up as effectively or last as long as the solid Teflon rings.

Special tools are required to install solid turbine-shaft Teflon sealing rings. These tools are somewhat expensive, but necessary to effectively install and resize the new rings. An option to buying the tools is to have a local transmission shop install the seals. Most shops will do so for a reasonable fee.

spacer. Install the friction and steel plates, alternating and ending up with a friction. Install the backing plate and snap ring, and check clutch-pack clearance. Once the input drum is fully assembled, air test the clutch packs through the three holes in the turbine shaft.

Install the original selective washer onto the input drum. Lubricate and install the Torrington bearing onto the turbine shaft resting against the selective washer. You are now ready to install the turbine-shaft solid-Teflon sealing rings.

Remove the old Teflon sealing rings. Early units used scarf-cut rings; later units used solid rings that require cutting them off with a sharp knife or razor blade.

Once all of the old Teflon sealing rings are removed, adjust the installation tool so that the bottom edge of the tool lines up with the lowest ring groove. Use plenty of clean ATF as a lubricant, and install the lowest sealing ring. Make sure to use even pressure with both hands as the new Teflon ring is slid into position.

The installation tool is adjustable and allows you to set the lower lip of the tool to facilitate the installation of each of the four solid Teflon sealing rings. Adjust the tool as shown, so the lip is lined up with the upper edge of the groove in the shaft.

Starting with the lower sealing ring first, carefully slide the sealing ring over the installation tool. Use plenty of clean ATF and keep the sealing ring as even as possible as it is slid into position. Gently push the sealing ring into the appropriate groove in the shaft, and adjust the tool for the next ring. Once all of the sealing rings are in place, gently push them into the grooves and allow them to relax for at least 15 minutes.

Using your thumbs and forefingers, gently push the sealing ring into the groove. It will have stretched out some from the installation process. Re-adjust the installation tool for the next ring groove, and repeat the installation process. Continue until all of the sealing rings have been installed into the grooves. Allow the rings to relax for at least 15 minutes. The rings are now ready to be re-sized. Lubricate the rings and resizing tool with a generous amount of clean ATF. Push each ring into the groove with your thumbs and forefingers. Gently work the resizing tool over the first ring.

Do not force the tool at any point or it will cut the ring. The tool has a smooth chamfered leading edge to facilitate seal installation. It may help to work the tool in a circular motion while applying slight down pressure. Once the tool has made it past the last seal, leave it in place for at least one hour to bring the rings back into shape. At this point in the rebuild, if there is no pressing emergency to get the transmission back into service, replace the plastic resizing tool with an old stator shaft, and leave it in place for 24 hours before finishing the rebuild.

If an old stator shaft was available and used to resize the Teflon turbine-shaft seals, it provides a good opportunity to air check the drum. By applying compressed air to the holes in the stator shaft, you can perform an air test of the clutch drums, and the sealing rings, at the same time.

Reverse Drum Rebuilding

The reverse drum is relatively easy to rebuild. There are two basic varieties. Early units used a steel piston and waved steel plate in the

The new sealing rings must be resized. Once they have been allowed to relax, gently push them into the grooves with your thumbs and forefingers, making a basic cloverleaf shape. As the resizing tool is pushed over each ring, it will force the rings into the grooves in the shaft. Use plenty of clean ATF as a lubricant, and never force the tool down over the rings; they are easily cut by the sharp edges of the grooves. It may help to rotate the resizing tool and turn it while pushing it down over the rings. Resize one ring at a time, and lift the tool up after the ring is forced into the groove, to make sure that it wasn't damaged. Once down over the last ring, leave the resizing tool in place for at least one hour.

You can also use your old stator shaft to air check the input-drum clutch packs and the sealing rings at the same time. Apply compressed air to the holes in the stator shaft as shown. You can also use the oil-pump assembly to accomplish the same task, by applying compressed air to the holes at the gasket surface where the oil pump meets the transmission case. Air checks are a very important part of transmission building, as they will locate problems before the transmission is fully assembled and placed in service. If problems develop with the transmission during your road test, at least you know that the clutch packs were applying and the seals were installed correctly.

An old stator shaft can be used as an effective tool to resize the solid Teflon sealing rings. It does not need to be removed from the oil pump. Use plenty of clean ATF as a lubricant. Install the stator shaft down over the seals, and if possible, leave it in place at least 24 hours. This will guarantee that the seals are effectively resized, and make the transmission much easier to assemble.

Use a spring compressor to compress the spring cage, and remove the snap ring. Remove the reverse drum from the spring compressor. The piston can be removed from the drum by applying compressed air to the feed hole, or simply dropping the drum a few inches down onto a wooden bench top.

Early units used a steel apply piston, and will have a check ball in the drum. Later units used an aluminum apply piston, and no check ball will be found in the drum. The size and shape of the feed hole in the drum may not be the same. If a new drum is being used, make sure that it has the same configuration as the one being replaced.

assembly. Later units used an aluminum piston with a Belleville steel apply plate. The early drums used a check ball in the drum; the later aluminum piston drums were of the feed-bleed design. Although no check ball was used in the drum, the aluminum apply piston has a small bleed hole instead. The reverse drum also does double duty, as it provides a surface where the band applies. Carefully inspect the surface of the drum. It should be clean, flat, and smooth. Resist any urge to sand the surface where the band applies. This can cause rough band engagement, erratic shift performance, and possible band failure.

Remove the backing-plate retaining ring, the backing plate, steels, clutches, and waved or beveled steel plate. Install the reverse drum in a vise and remove the snap ring over the spring cage. Remove the spring

I recommend reducing the bleed-hole diameter in the aluminum apply piston. The restrictor is installed as shown in the pictures. These restrictors are available through most transmission parts suppliers, and are included in many aftermarket shift kits.

cage and apply piston. Identify the type of apply piston, either aluminum or steel. If an aluminum piston is used, it is recommended to reduce the size of the bleed hole. These restrictors are available through most transmission parts suppliers and come in many aftermarket shift kits.

I recommend replacing the upper and lower bushings in the reverse drum. Collapse the upper bushing

The upper bushing should be collapsed until it can be pried easily from the drum. The upper edge of the bushing is higher than the drum's surface. Use a sharp punch to catch the edge of the bushing with the punch and collapse the bushing in two or three places. Pry it off the drum. Check to make sure that the surface under the bushing wasn't damaged by the punch. If so, gently sand out any nicks with fine auto-body sandpaper prior to driving in a new bushing.

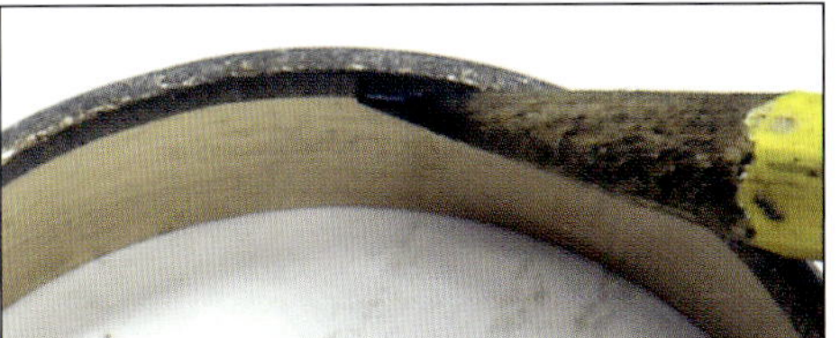

The upper bushing has a chamfered inner edge. This chamfered area must be installed facing away from the drum. This allows solid Teflon sealing rings to slide past the bushing when the oil pump is installed.

Clean the clutch drum, apply piston, spring cage, and snap ring. Once the drum is clean, drive in a new upper and lower bushing. Also, check the drum surface where the band applies—it should be smooth and free of nicks and gouges. Avoid any temptation to sand the drum where the band applies. This can cause shift-performance problems, and can even damage the lining on the band.

with a sharp punch and pry it out of the housing. Install the upper bushing with the chamfered inside edge facing upward. The lower bushing is driven in flush with the housing; it is not chamfered on either end.

Clean the reverse drum, apply piston, spring cage, and snap ring. Install new lip seals on the apply piston. Lubricate the seals and the drum with clean ATF and install the piston into the housing. Compress the spring cage and install the snap ring.

Install the Belleville plate, then the steels, clutches, and backing plate. Start with a steel on top of the Belleville plate, then alternate friction, steel, friction, steel, and end with the thick backing plate. Install the snap ring. The drum can be air checked through one of the oil-supply feed holes, or through

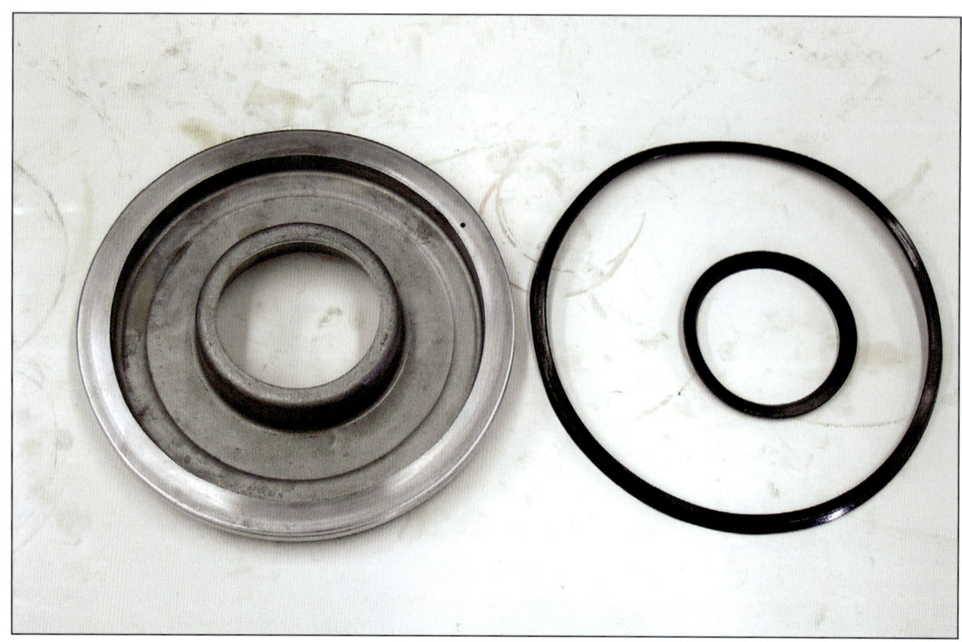

Install new lip seals onto the apply piston. The lips on the seals face go down or away from the open end of the drum. The steel apply piston takes a smaller outer lip seal than the aluminum piston. Most rebuild kits for the 4L60 transmissions will contain both lip seals. Make sure to compare the new seal with the one removed.

The factory provided a very generous wide and smooth chamfered area to facilitate easy seal installation. It still helps to use your special tool to help get the seals started. Use plenty of clean ATF, and turn the piston while gently pushing it down into the drum.

Several different servos were used to apply the band. The smaller servo is from a Corvette, and is preferred since its greater surface area provides more holding power to the band. The aftermarket also has even larger servos available, for even more holding power. I consider the Corvette servo fine for most high-performance rebuilds.

the case passage once installed in the transmission.

The servo to apply the band is located in the case, under the servo cover. The servo's entire surface area is used for fourth-gear application, the inner piston areas for the 1-2 shifts. Several different servo-piston assemblies were used through the years of production. High-performance and Corvette applications received the best arrangement. The Corvette servo is available from the aftermarket, and is recommended for all performance levels.

The servo assembly can be installed at this time. If you are installing an aftermarket shift kit, follow the shift-kit directions exactly, as they may replace parts in the servo assembly, or deviate from the factory arrangement of the components. Shift kits may also require that you reduce the band apply-pin length to accommodate their installation. You may also be installing a Corvette or aftermarket servo. Rebuild kits come with the scarf-cut Teflon seals for all of the factory servos that were used through the years

The aluminum apply piston requires a Belleville plate. Install the Belleville plate as shown, with curvature down against the apply piston. For any early drum with a steel apply piston, a waved plate is used instead, and it can be installed in any position.

Install the clutch pack on top of the Belleville plate as shown. Start with a steel plate, then a friction, and alternate steel, friction, steel, friction, ending with the backing plate. Make sure to install the flat side of the thick steel backing plate down against the top friction plate. Install the snap ring and make sure that the clutch pack has some clearance.

Our reverse drum is completely assembled and ready to install. It can be air tested through the oil-feed supply holes, or through the case passage under the valve body once the transmission is assembled.

The servo assembly should be installed as a unit. Use plenty of TransGel on the outer O-rings. The servo is pushed into place, and the large metal retaining ring is snapped into the case.

Compressed air can be applied to the exhaust hole at the oil-pan mounting surface as shown, to apply the 2-4 band. This test checks for correct servo operation and makes sure the band is getting a sufficient hold on the reverse drum. Listen for air leaks and make sure that the reverse drum will not turn when the band is fully applied.

of production. Once the servo and retaining ring are in place, you can air test the band by applying compressed air to the exhaust hole at the transmission-pan mounting surface. The pan gasket is cut out at this area to expose the hole.

Oil Pump Rebuilding

The oil pump is the heart of the transmission. It must be completely and correctly rebuilt to ensure correct transmission function, as it supplies the needed flow and pressure to all of the components.

As with other areas of the 4L60 transmissions, the oil pump would undergo several changes through the years of production. The biggest problem area with very early units was the front seal blowing out of the housing, and the bushing moving forward. The housings were redesigned with a lip to retain the front bushing, a larger oil drain-back hole, and a retainer over the front seal.

The pump rotor was also upgraded from the original 7-vane design, to 10 vanes, then 13 vanes. The 10- and 13-vane rotors do not increase the oil-pump output or pressure. They were used to help smooth out the oil flow and reduce pulsation.

Early oil pumps with the 7-vane rotors also used “soft” pump rings, which were known for breaking and causing complete transmission failure. Always install hardened rings into any transmission made before the auxiliary valve-body 1987 units.

Although it contains quite a few parts, the oil pump is relatively easy to rebuild. Remove the five bolts and separate the pump halves. Once you have separated your pump halves, remove the rotor, pump rings, vanes, and plastic rotor guide. Remove the priming spring(s), the outer pump slide, and the slide pin. Don’t forget

The oil drain-back hole in the pump should be enlarged to 5⁄16 in diameter. This will ensure that oil pressure doesn’t build up behind the front seal and push it out of the housing. It is fine if part of the new bushing blocks some of the oil hole. Note that the later pump as shown has a lip just below the oil drain-back hole to keep the bushing from moving forward. Early pumps will not have this lip.

The later model 4L60E units used a 13-vane oil-pump assembly. They also used hardened rings, and double springs for the pump slide. The 13-vane pumps do not pump more oil than earlier 7- or 10-vane designs. In contrast, the vanes take up more room, and pump output would probably be less than earlier pumps. The number of vanes used in the pump was increased to smooth out the oil flow and minimize pulsations, not to increase oil flow or line pressure.

If a small ⅜-in impact is available, remove the oil-pump attaching bolts. The oil pump can be difficult to hold if a ratchet is used to remove the bolts.

The oil-pump slide springs should be removed first, to take pressure off of the pump slide to facilitate removing the pump internals. Some early oil pumps will only use one pump-slide spring, but the double-spring setup is highly recommended; these parts are available separately, and a new inner spring is supplied in most aftermarket shift kits.

about the tiny spring under the pin. Under the pump slide is a metal ring with a very thin O-ring under it. A small magnet may be required to remove the metal ring to replace the O-ring. The front pump section will require a new seal and bushing. Remove the seal by collapsing it with a sharp punch, and drive the bushing out of the housing. It is a good habit to always drive the bushing down from the seal end, as later pumps use a lip to keep the bushing from moving forward.

Once the pump halves are thoroughly cleaned, carefully inspect all parts for wear or damage. The vane-type oil pump is an excellent design, but lacks the ability to ingest a lot of dirt or debris. The metal vanes ride directly on the machined aluminum surfaces of the pump halves. These surfaces must be in excellent condition, without scratches or gouges, or oil-pump efficiency and longevity will be affected. Once all components

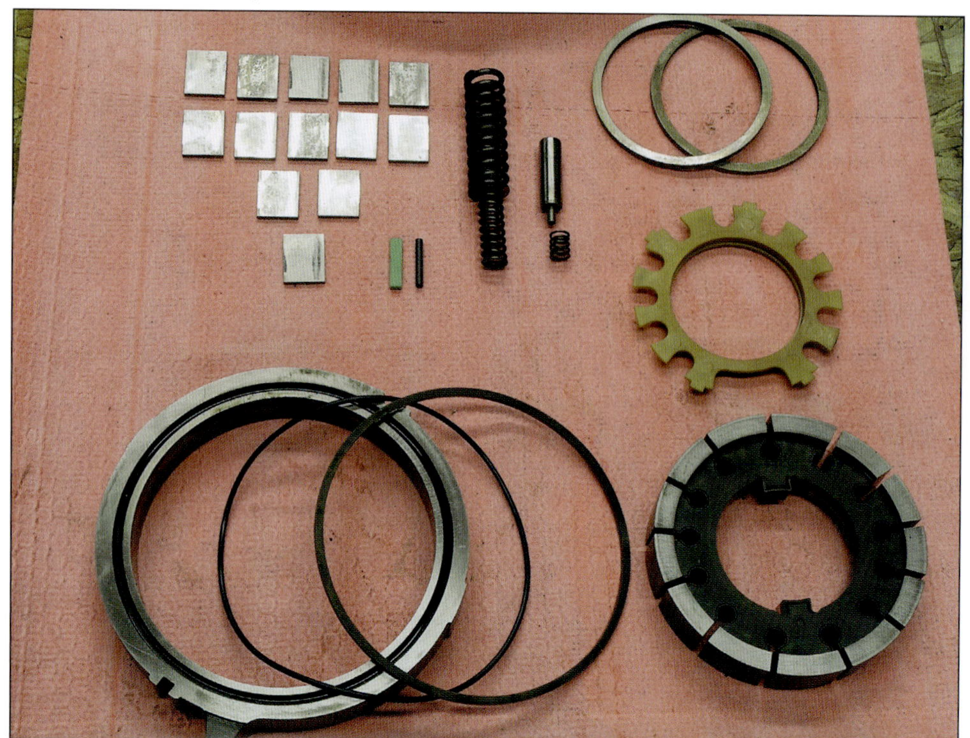

The oil-pump internal components should be cleaned and inspected. The back edges of the pump vanes will often be worn where they contact the pump rings. Early oil pumps used pump rings that were known for cracking or breaking, causing complete transmission failure. Always install late-style hardened pump rings for any rebuild. Pump vanes, slides, and rotors are available separately, or as a service package from most transmission-parts suppliers. If you have an early 7-vane pump, this is a good time to upgrade to a later 10-vane pump, with hardened rings and double pump-slide springs.

Always drive the bushing down away from the seal side of the housing. Later oil pumps will have a small groove cast into them, designed to keep the bushing from moving forward.

pass a visual inspection, you are ready to start assembling the oil pump.

The front bushing is installed first. Drive the bushing in from the bottom, and gently seat it against the lip in the housing. With early oil pumps that do not have the retaining lip, drive the new bushing flush with the inner edge of the housing. Once your new bushing is in place, it is a good idea to test fit the bushing onto the torque

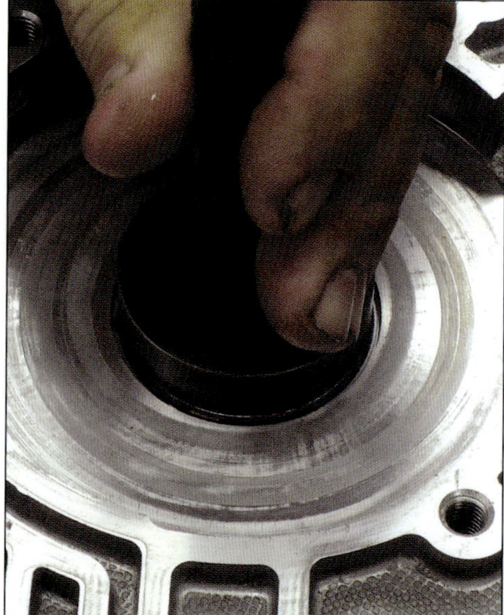

Apply a small bead of red Loctite to the new bushing. Drive the bushing into position. If the pump has a retaining lip, gently seat the new bushing against the lip.

It is a good idea to test fit the front bushing before completing the transmission build. Use the torque converter that is going to be used with the transmission. Some aftermarket torque converters will be slightly larger in diameter at the hub than factory converters. Lubricate the bushing with ATF or TransGel and slide it over the torque converter. It should turn freely without any tight spots. The bushing has a very soft outer surface. If there are any tight spots they will be visible on the surface. If the bushing was driven in correctly, and not up over the retaining lip in the pump housing, it should turn freely on the torque-converter hub. Minor tight spots can be sanded out with very fine auto-body sandpaper. If the bushing is not straight in the housing, or driven up over the lip and binding on the torque-converter hub, remove it and install a new bushing.

Obtain a suitable tool to drive in the front seal. Here, an old valve is being used. Apply some Loctite to the seal, and drive it in until seated. Do not drive the seal so hard that the inner spring on the lip seal comes off.

The oil pump slide is installed first. Make sure to replace the thin O-ring on the backside of the slide, under the metal ring. Retain both parts with TransGel while installing the pump slide. Install the small rubber spacer and Teflon slide first. The guide pin and spring go in next, followed by the slide springs. Make sure that the Teflon slide and rubber spacer are flush with the top edge of the pump slide.

converter. Install the front bushing with a suitable tool that will seat it evenly against the pump housing.

Once you have the front seal and bushing installed in the housing, you can begin oil-pump assembly. Vane and pump-rotor kits are available if you want to upgrade from a 7-vane to a 10-vane pump. With any upgrade, the pump rings are the most important. Having more vanes in the pump assembly will not increase oil flow or improve oil-pump efficiency. Attempting to use the early soft rings with any pump will most likely result in oil-pump failure. Aftermarket high-performance pump rings are available from several sources, and are highly recommended. Vane kits are available as service packages, if you want to re-use the stock rotor assembly and simply install new vanes.

Install a new O-ring into the groove in the bottom of the pump slide, and retain it with a dab of transmission gel. Install the thin metal pump guide ring over the new O-ring, and install the slide into the upper half of the oil pump. The pump slide is retained by a pin on one side, and uses a Teflon slide backed by a small rubber sleeve. Install the pump slide springs.

Some early transmissions only use one pump-slide spring; both

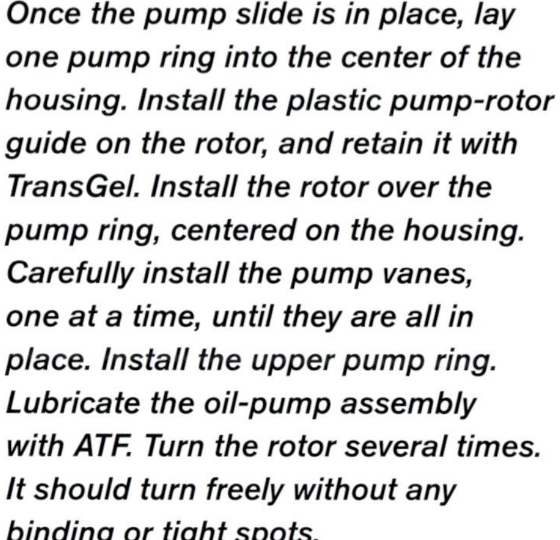

Once the pump slide is in place, lay one pump ring into the center of the housing. Install the plastic pump-rotor guide on the rotor, and retain it with TransGel. Install the rotor over the pump ring, centered on the housing. Carefully install the pump vanes, one at a time, until they are all in place. Install the upper pump ring. Lubricate the oil-pump assembly with ATF. Turn the rotor several times. It should turn freely without any binding or tight spots.

Install a new bushing into the stator shaft. Most new stator shafts will not *come with a bushing. If this bushing is left out, the turbine shaft will wear out the Teflon rings quickly, and damage both the turbine shaft and the inside of the stator.*

springs are available separately and most shift kits will come with a new inner spring. Install a pump ring, pump rotor, rotor guide, pump vanes, and second pump ring.

Remove and replace the stator bushings before bolting the pump halves together. Line up the two pump halves and install the bolts finger tight. Use a band to align the pump halves, and tighten the bolts. Remove and replace the filter assembly, and install a new thrust washer. You are now ready to install the Teflon sealing rings into the grooves on the stator shaft.

Installing one-piece Teflon sealing rings for the reverse drum is highly recommended. The factory used scarf-cut rings for the early units, then upgraded to the one-piece rings to improve reverse-drum

Install a new filter screen into the pump housing. Make sure to install a new O-ring on the filter housing, and lubricate it with a drop of ATF or TransGel.

Carefully line up the pump halves and install the five attaching bolts. Tighten them finger tight only. Install a band to line up the pump halves. A Phillips screwdriver can be used to line up the oil holes between the pump halves. Once the pump halves are lined up, tighten the bolts to 15 to 18 ft-lbs. A high quality ⅜-in impact can be carefully set to tighten the bolts, as the pump is very difficult to hold if you are working by yourself.

performance and long-term reliability. The installation process is similar to installing solid Teflon rings on the turbine shaft. The solid rings will provide a positive seal at the reverse drum, and are very durable. Most rebuild kits for the 4L60 transmissions will come with scarf-cut rings; kits for the 4L60E transmissions come with solid rings, and many kits come with both.

Install the outer pump seal into the groove on the pump housing. For the 4L60E transmissions, install a new seal into the housing for the oil filter.

The oil-pump assembly is now complete. If removed for cleaning or shift-kit installation, install the pressure-regulator valve assembly and the TCC valve. It is recommended to

Continued on page 70

One-piece Teflon seals are used on the later transmissions, and are highly recommended for all units. To install the later one-piece Teflon seals, special tools—similar to those used for the turbine-shaft Teflon seals—are required. The new one-piece seals are pushed into position over a plastic guide, and then resized. Line up the lower part of the installation tool with the lower seal groove. Apply a generous amount of clean ATF to the tool and the Teflon seal, and push it into place. Adjust the tool for the upper groove, and repeat the procedure. Once both seals are in place, allow them to relax for about 15 minutes. Carefully push them into the grooves with your thumbs and forefingers. Gently slide the resizing tools down over the seals. It may help to work the tool in a circular motion while turning and pushing it down gently at the same time. Do not force the resizing tool over the seals. The sharp groove edges will easily cut them. Once the resizing tools are down over both seals, leave them in place at least one hour. If there is no big hurry to finish the build, leave them in place for 24 hours. The pump Teflon seals should be left off of the pump if we are installing and removing the pump to check input-shaft endplay. The tools to install solid Teflon rings are somewhat expensive, but worth the additional cost. Most transmission shops will install the seals for you for a small fee so you can avoid buying the tools.

Install a new outer pump seal into the groove in the oil pump. Apply TransGel to the seal before attempting to install the oil pump into the transmission case. The seal should be left off of the pump if we are installing and removing the pump to check input-shaft endplay. Make sure to install the seal for final pump installation.

4L60E transmissions used a different filter seal with a hard metal housing. Carefully collapse the housing with a sharp punch, and pry off the old seal. Drive a new seal into place with the correct size bushing driver.

The pressure regulator valve and TCC valve should be removed from the oil pump for cleaning. Many aftermarket shift kits will supply a new pressure-regulator spring to install. Both of these valves can be accessed with the oil pump installed in the transmission. However, it is simply easier to remove them while the pump is apart by gently clamping the oil pump in a soft-jawed vise, and removing the snap rings that retain the valves.

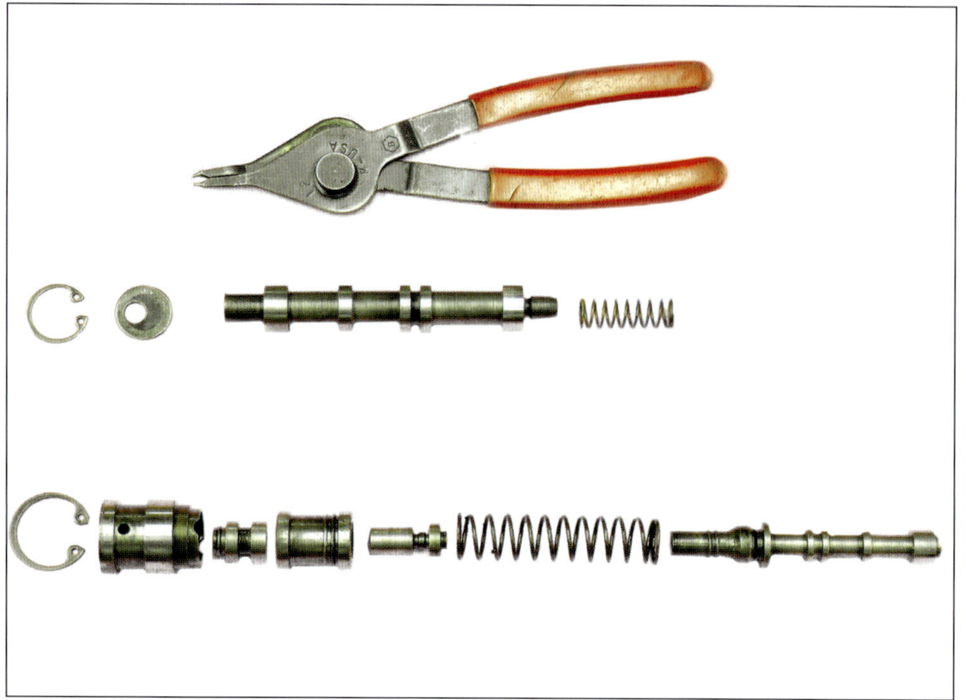

The TCC (torque converter clutch) valve (top) and PR (pressure regulator) valve (bottom) have been removed from the oil pump. Use a slight amount of TransGel to keep the PR valve and related components from falling apart when reassembling them into the housing. The parts must be installed as shown, and the snap ring should be fully seated to effectively hold them in place. The PR valve from a 4L60E transmission is slightly different, but is in the same location and is removed in the same manner as the PR valve from a 4L60 unit.

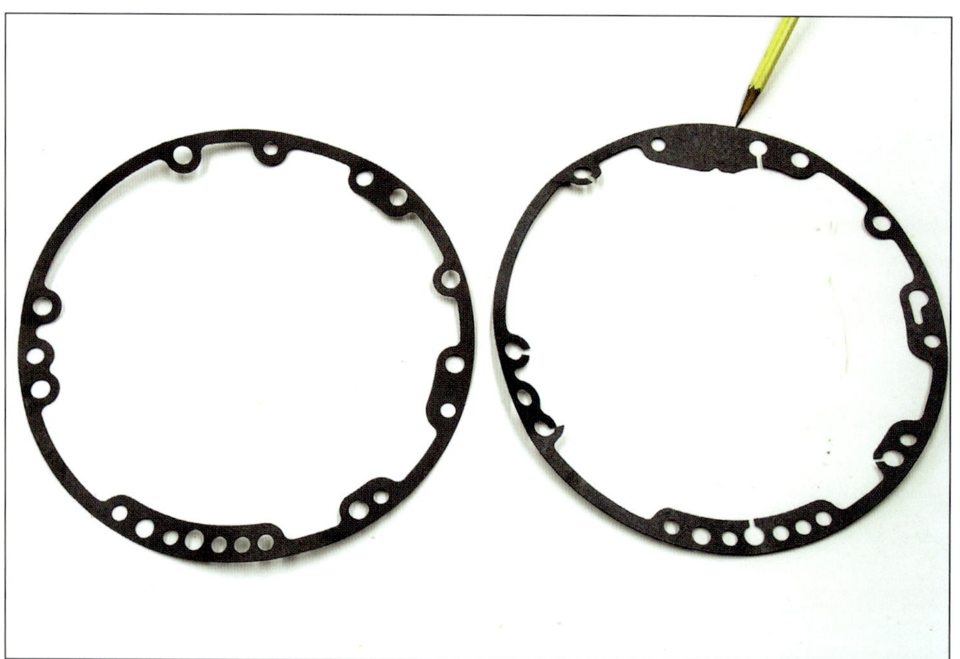

Two different pump-to-case gaskets are used; 1987 and later units used the gasket on the right.

leave the resizing tool in place for at least an hour. If there is no big hurry to finish the transmission build, leave the resizing tool in place overnight. The reverse drum can also be installed over the Teflon rings to help resize them; however, it can be difficult to remove, as the pump rings can catch on the lower edge of the reverse-drum front bushing.

Our oil pump is now ready to install. Make sure to put the gasket in place. There are two different oil pump-to-case gaskets. Units made in and after 1987 use the later design. Use at least two guide studs to facilitate oil-pump installation. Lubricate the outer pump seal and the case with TransGel or ATF. Install the oil pump—it can be tapped gently into place with a soft-faced mallet. Do

Our final air check is done through the passages in the transmission after the pump is installed into the case. We can apply all the clutch packs and listen for air leaks. The band can also be applied through the exhaust hole on the flat surface where the oil pan mounts.

Replacing the Stator Shaft

Replacing the stator shaft is relatively easy. The most difficult part is removing the three Torx-head attaching screws.

Most Torx sockets are too fragile to effectively remove the screws. If they will not come out, cut a slot in them with a thin cut-off wheel on an angle grinder. Use an impact driver and large flat blade, and they will come right out. The stator can be pressed out, or driven out with a large hammer and suitable flat-faced driver. Make sure the new replacement stator shaft has a bushing installed.

There may not be one installed, and leaving it out will destroy the turbine shaft in short order once the transmission is placed in service.

The stator is pressed into the oil pump and secured with three Torx-head screws. They can be very difficult to remove. An impact driver is usually required to get them out of the pump.

The stator shaft uses two bushings. If a new stator shaft is purchased, it may not have the bushings in place.

Install the manual-shaft seal into the case. Any suitable socket or large punch will work; just make sure not to hit the seal so hard that it crushes the metal shell.

The manual shaft should be de-burred prior to installation. There will be a sharp knife-edge just above the threads. This could cut the seal as it passes through it, and cause an oil leak.

not force the pump into place. Install the pump bolts with new O-rings (early models used flat sealing washers). Make sure the input shaft turns, and verify the endplay.

Using compressed air through the appropriate passages in the case, you can test the operation of the reverse clutch, forward, overrunning, and 3-4 clutch pack. These were already bench tested. Testing them through the case simply ensures that

Testing Clutch Packs

Prior to installation into the transmission case, you can check the operation of the reverse, overrunning, forward, and 3-4 clutch packs. This will require gently clamping the oil pump stator side down into a soft-jawed vise. Install the reverse drum and input drum onto the pump. Using the appropriate holes in the oil pump, test the operation of the clutch packs using compressed air.

An air-gun tip with a rubber seal, or a shop rag to prevent air leakage at the supply holes, is helpful. Up to this point, all the drums should have been air checked separately. This final check ensures that you have a good seal between the Teflon seals and the oil pump, as well as at the clutch-pack apply pistons.

The oil pump can be gently clamped in a soft-jawed vise, with the reverse and input drums, to facilitate air checking these components for correct function prior to installing them in the case. Air is applied through the appropriate holes in the oil pump to apply the clutch packs.

you have not damaged any sealing rings during installation of the pump, and have a good seal between the pump and the transmission case.

Valve Body and Related Parts

Install a new seal for the manual shaft into the case. Before attempting to install the manual shaft, deburr the leading edge so it doesn't cut the seal lip when installed. Install the manual valve into the case; lubricate the seal with Trans-Gel. Install the rooster comb and rod for the parking pawl. Use a drop of Loctite on the nut and tighten it with a large wrench. Install the spacer spring and the hood over the parking pawl. Test the parking pawl for full engagement by attempting to turn the output shaft with the parking pawl fully engaged.

Install the wiring harness for 4L60E models at this time. It is not accessible once the valve body is in place. A new wiring harness is highly recommended. The wiring harness

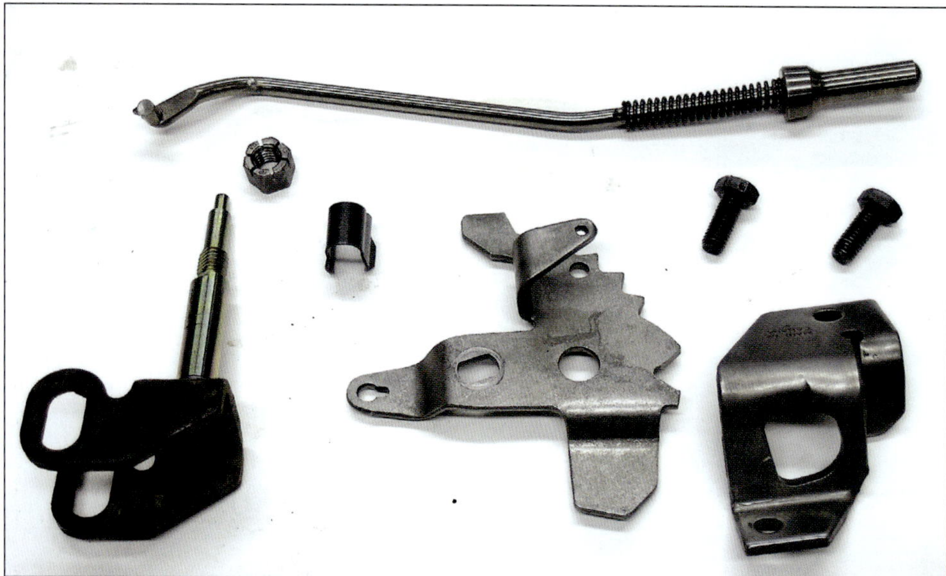

The components of the manual shaft and parking-pawl rod are shown in the picture on the left. The manual shaft holds the rooster comb, and is retained with a nut. Make sure to tighten the nut securely, and then snap the spacer into place as shown. The parking-pawl rod is positioned as shown, and then the retainer is bolted into place. Operate the manual shaft several times while turning the output shaft to make sure that the parking pawl fully engages. Perform this test again once the valve body and leaf spring are bolted into place. When the manual shaft is moved into the highest or Park position, the pawl should fully engage and the output shaft should be locked in position.

The early-style accumulator pistons (right) used solid Teflon seals. They should be replaced with the later-style pistons, and new rubber seals installed. Also check the pistons for excessive clearance where they slide over the pins, and replace as needed.

can hang out of the case so it will not interfere with other component installation. Install the 3-4 accumulator pistons with a new seal. Replace the early-style pistons that used Teflon seals with the later design.

Check your shift-kit directions if one is being installed, and use the recommended accumulator spring from the kit—and any recommended restrictors—to drive into the accumulator feed hole in the case.

After the manual shaft is inserted into the transmission case, the rooster comb is installed on the shaft, and retained with a nut. A long tapered punch or screwdriver can be used to hole the shift linkage while the nut is being tightened (top photo). Next, snap the spacer into place between the rooster comb and the transmission case (center photo). Install the return spring on the parking pawl (bottom left photo), then install the retainer and tighten the bolts securely. Note the position of the parking pawl (bottom right photo). Operate the manual shaft several times while turning the output shaft to make sure that the parking pawl fully engages. Perform this test again once the valve body and leaf spring are bolted into place. When the manual shaft is moved into the highest, or "Park," position, the pawl should fully engage and the output shaft should be locked in position. The parking pawl should move out of position and disengage, allowing the output shaft to turn freely in all other positions.

Install the case check balls—for stock builds install in the locations where removed. For shift kits follow the shift-kit directions exactly. Install the 3-4 accumulator piston, pin, and spring into the case. Make sure to use the late-style piston and install a new rubber seal. Closely inspect the separator plate for damage to the holes for the steel check balls. Repair or replace the separator plate as needed.

Make sure to use the correct gasket between the separator plate and the case. Most rebuild kits will contain several different gaskets, and instructions as to which ones to use for various models. Install the 1-2 accumulator housing with a new seal on the piston, and a new spring if one is supplied with a shift kit.

Install the auxiliary valve body if building a 1987–1992 4L60 unit. Make sure to remove the piston inside the auxiliary valve body and install a new seal. Replace the spring for the piston if broken—a problem occasionally encountered with these units. *A broken spring may have damaged the sealing surface, requiring replacement of the unit.*

Install the retaining plate on pre-1987 models. Install the check

The valve-body gasket that goes against the case will have a large "C" on it. Make sure to install the steel check balls in the case first. Apply a small amount of TransGel to the gasket to keep it in place. The TransGel will hold the gasket in place while the separator plate and upper gasket are installed.

The separator plate is installed next, with a gasket between it and the valve body. Again, apply some TransGel to both sides of the plate to hold the gaskets in place. The upper gasket will have a "V" on it, indicating it goes against the valve body.

Install the 1-2 accumulator housing.

balls into the correct valve-body locations, and retain with TransGel. Gently guide the valve body into place and finger tighten the bolts. Make sure to use the correct gasket between the valve body and the separator plate. The spool-valve link will need to be attached to the hole in the rooster comb as the valve body is lowered.

Tighten all of the valve-body bolts, working from the center to the outside in a circular pattern. Do not over-tighten the bolts, and make sure to use the correct length bolts on the 4L60E models. Using the long bolts in the wrong locations can damage the transmission and prevent it from working once placed in service. Install the lock-up solenoid and the wiring harness. Install and hook up the temperature switch (if used) and any other pressure switches. It is always recommended to install a new lock-up solenoid for all rebuilds. At a minimum apply 12 volts to the old valve with a good ground and check for correct operation. A distinct audible "click" when voltage is applied to the valve indicates it is working correctly.

1987 and later 4L60 transmissions used an auxiliary valve body and oil tube running up to the pump. The oil tube is retained at the auxiliary valve-body end by a small retainer under a bolt, and the tube uses another retainer under a valve-body bolt, as shown.

All 4L60 models used a TV (throttle valve) cable to operate the throttle valve. The TV cable provides the reference signal to the transmission. Using the governor to determine vehicle speed, the TV valve adjustment is critical for correct transmission operation. There is no vacuum signal used on 4L60 transmissions to a vacuum modulator to help control shift function reached third and/or fourth gear.

Valve-body bolts should not be over-tightened, as the threads in the case can be stripped out. Cutting off most of the handle of a ⅜-in ratchet will prevent over-torquing the bolts.

For non-electronic models, install the TV cable and its associated hardware on the valve body. Make sure to install a new seal where the cable seats to the case. The oil filter is last on the list. A new seal is installed in the pump. The later models used a lip seal with a steel outer shell. Early models used a multiple lip seal. A multiple lip seal is also used for the dipstick tube, and should be installed into the case prior to installing the tube.

Thoroughly clean the transmission pan and seal surface. The oil pans are reinforced and seldom give any trouble with leaks. Do not use any gasket sealer on the transmission mating surface. A very small amount of RTV can be used to hold the gasket in place on the pan. Several different types of pan gaskets are

4L60 transmissions used the seal for the filter shown on the right. The 4L60E units use a lip-type seal molded to a metal housing that is driven into the oil pump, seen on the left.

The rear seal is driven in flush with the end of the tail housing. Any large flat driver, even a block of wood, can be used to drive the seal in place.

Make sure to install the large square-cut seal onto the tail housing before bolting it to the transmission. This is the same seal used by TH350 transmissions, and has proven to be a very good, leak-free design.

available. Cork is the most common —the fiber gasket is preferred, as it will not smash out and tear as easily if the bolts are over-tightened.

The tail housing is next. Remove the old seal from the housing with a seal remover. It can also be removed by driving the seal housing in with a large punch or screwdriver in three places. It will just about fall out after doing this. Drive out the bushing and install a new bushing and seal. Use a drop of Loctite to retain them. Install a new seal on the tail housing and bolt it onto the transmission. Make sure to install any reluctors (if removed) or speedometer drive gears onto the tail shaft before installing the tail housing. Install the speedometer driven-gear housing using a new outer O-ring and new speedometer-gear seal. Many of the housings were made of plastic—inspect closely for cracks in the housing prior to installing it.

A spinner wrench is used to tighten the oil-pan bolts. They only need to be tight enough to compress the gasket. Over-tightening the bolts can cause the gasket to separate and leak.

Thoroughly clean the governor and make sure it operates freely. The weights and center section should move freely without binding. Lubricate it with clean ATF only. Inspect the drive gear, replace if worn or damaged. Install the governor into the case. Install the governor cover with a new seal. The governor cover needs to be driven in place, use a large flat punch and carefully drive the cover in place till it's flush on all sides.

Install the transmission mount, and torque the bolts as required. Remove the transmission from the holding fixture and place it down on a suitable flat surface resting on the oil pan. Any external linkage or

Install a new O-ring on the speedometer housing, and new inner seal and metal clip retainer. Some housings will use a lip-type seal molded to a metal shell. These seals are not provided in most rebuild kits, and may require replacement of the entire housing if the lip seal is damaged or worn.

Closely inspect the drive gear on the governor for wear or damaged teeth. They are relatively easy to replace. If a new gear is required, simply drive out the roll pin and pull the gear off the governor. The new gear is simply pressed into place by hand, and drilled for a new roll pin.

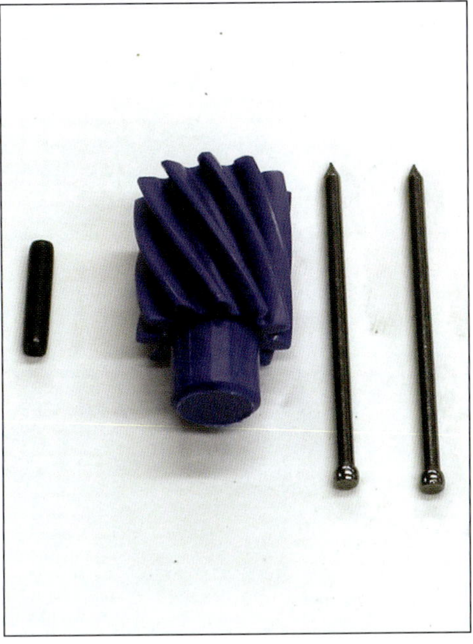

If the governor gear is worn or damaged it must be replaced. New gears are available. They come with a new roll pin and pins for the governor weights. The new gear will not be drilled for the pin. It must be pressed into position and drilled prior to driving in the roll pin.

other items removed from the case should be installed at this time. Check the cooling-line connections for damaged threads or nicks to the sealing surface for the flared cooling lines. Replace as needed.

Prior to installing the transmission, test fit the torque converter. A new converter should always be installed. The torque converter may be slightly difficult to install, as there will be minimum clearance at the new pump bushing, but it should go all the way back and engage with the oil-pump rotor. Make sure the torque converter is fully engaged and spins freely. Remove the converter and pour at least one quart of ATF slowly into it. It can now be reinstalled on the transmission. Your transmission is now ready to install in the vehicle.

The torque converter should be fitted into the transmission to make sure that it fully seats into the turbine shaft, stator shaft, and oil pump. If a new bushing was installed in the oil pump, the converter may be somewhat difficult to get into the transmission, as the clearance at the bushing will be minimal. The best method to install the converter is to lubricate the oil-pump drive, add at least 1 quart of ATF to the converter, and slide it into place while spinning it by hand. The converter is correctly installed when it engages the oil pump. There will be approximately ¼ in of clearance between the back of the torque converter and the transmission oil pump, when the torque converter is fully engaged in the oil pump. It is important to note here that any attempt to bolt the transmission to the engine when the torque converter is not fully seated in the oil pump will destroy the oil pump and possibly damage the oil-pump drive end of the torque converter.

Shift Kits

Several companies offer shift kits for the 4L60 transmissions; however, installing a shift kit can be a detailed and complicated process. Shift kits are designed to reprogram the shifting of the transmission. They do so by controlling the flow rate, pressure, and timing to the various components of the transmission. By sequencing the flow to the components, shift kits can control the shift firmness, improve holding power of the clutch packs, and improve the durability, performance, and longevity of the transmission.

Quite a few different shift kits are available for the 4L60 and 4L60E transmissions. They come with quite a few items to install, and with complete and detailed instructions. Be ready to spend as much or more time installing the shift kit as it took to completely rebuild the transmission.

For the purpose of this publication, it would be difficult to lay out the specific installation of each and every shift kit for these transmissions, as there are at least a dozen currently available. Instead, I will go over general guidelines for shift-kit installation, and helpful tips and procedures to make the process easier.

Before selecting and installing a shift kit, you need to decide if one is really needed. If you are building a transmission that has just led a long and healthy life behind a stock or nearly stock application, and simply requires rebuilding due to the transmission being worn out, a shift kit may not be required. If you thought that the shift performance of your transmission was not up to par before deciding to rebuild it, then a shift kit

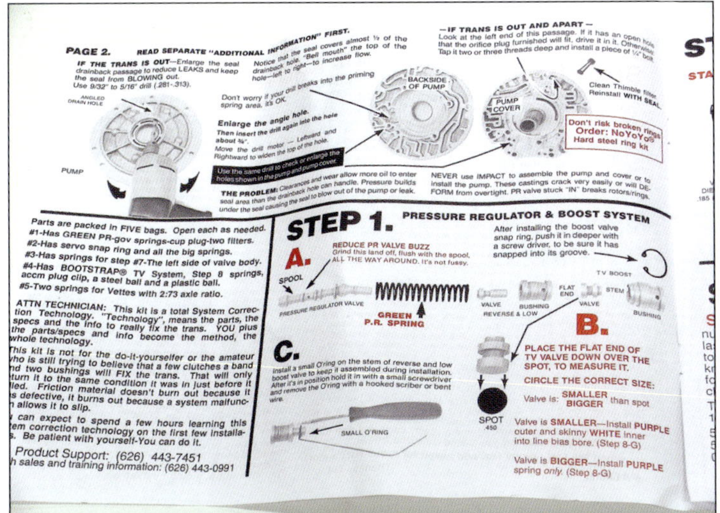

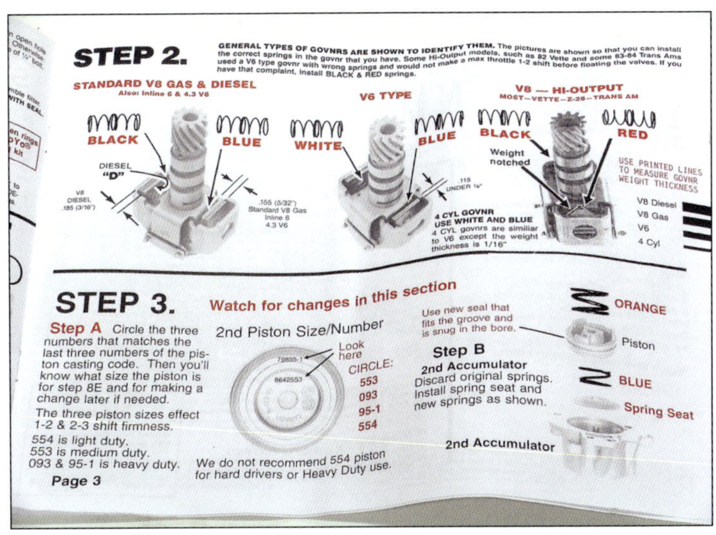

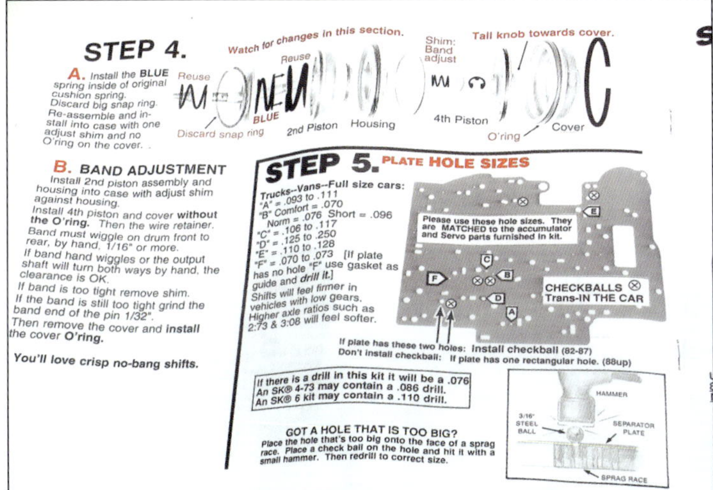

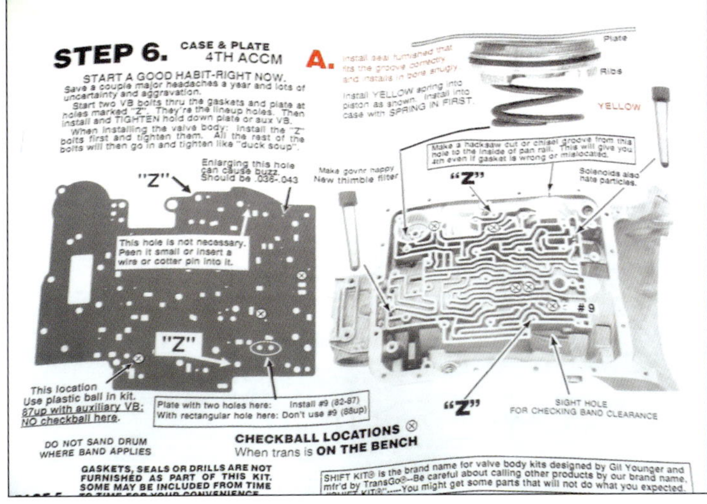

Read the instructions provided with your shift kit completely before rebuilding the transmission. Many shift kits also contain recommended upgrades, recommendations for clutch-pack clearances, band-to-pin clearance, and other helpful hints to use when rebuilding the transmission. They also have diagrams of the transmission case and separator plate and valve body, pointing out check-ball locations. Follow the directions for check-ball locations exactly for the model and year of transmission that you are working on. Fully expect to spend more time installing the shift kit than you did rebuilding the transmission.

would be a good idea. A shift kit should always be considered if you have purchased a used transmission of unknown origin, and are retro-fitting it into an older car, especially if the engine is making a lot of power.

Each manufacturer provides detailed and specific instructions for the correct installation of its shift kit. The installer must be fully prepared to spend as much or more time installing the shift kit as they did rebuilding the transmission. The shift-kit directions should be read in their entirety before rebuilding the transmission. There may be several modifications recommended or required to internal components of the transmission during the rebuilding process. This may include recommendations to install solid Teflon sealing rings, a restrictor into the aluminum reverse apply-piston bleed hole, etc.

Follow the shift-kit directions exactly. Although some builders and highly experienced hobbyists may make their own modifications in conjunction with certain shift kits, such as using custom separator-plate hole sizes or disabling accumulators, doing so is not recommended. Some shift kits will

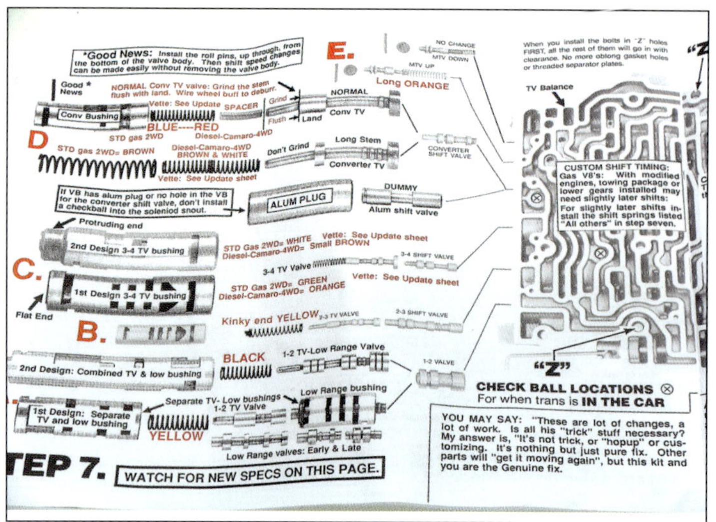

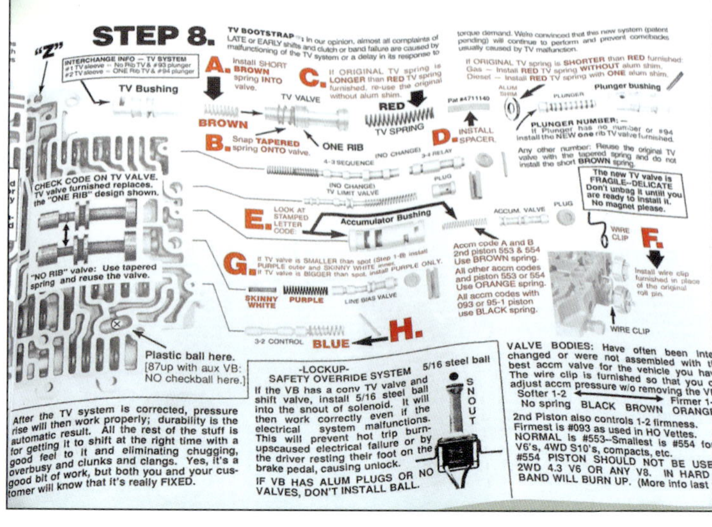

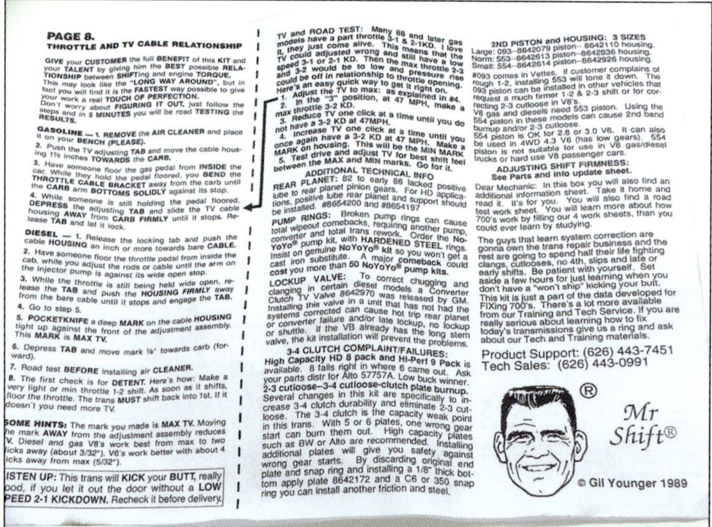
PAGE 8.

THROTTLE AND TV CABLE RELATIONSHIP

Product Support: (626) 443-7451
Tech Sales: (626) 443-0991

Mr Shift®

© Gil Younger 1989

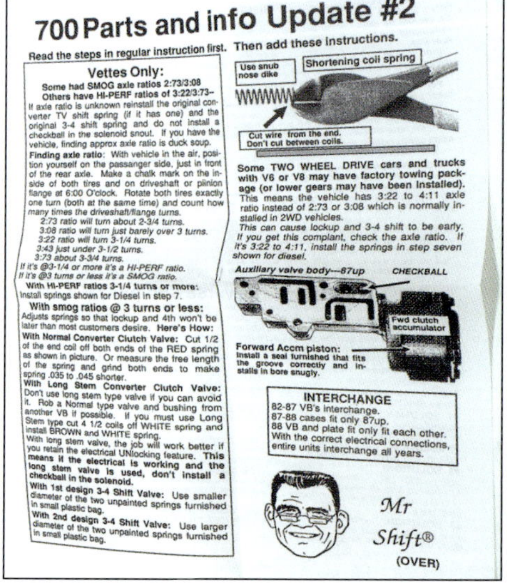
700 Parts and info Update #2

Read the steps in regular instruction first. Then add these instructions.

Vettes Only:

Some had SMOG axle ratios 2:73/3:08
Others have HI-PERF ratios of 3:22/3:73--
If axle ratio is unknown reinstall the original converter TV shift spring (if it has one) and the original 3-4 shift spring and do not install a checkball in the solenoid snout. If you have the vehicle, finding approx axle ratio is duck soup.

Finding axle ratio: With vehicle in the air, position yourself on the passanger side, just in front of the rear axle. Make a chalk mark on the inside of both tires and on driveshaft or piinion flange at 6:00 O'clock. Rotate both tires exactly one turn (both at the same time) and count how many times the driveshaft/flange turns.

2:73 ratio will turn about 2-3/4 turns.
3:08 ratio will turn just barely over 3 turns.
3:22 ratio will turn 3-1/4 turns.
3:43 just under 3-1/2 turns.
3:73 about 3-3/4 turns.

If it's @3-1/4 or more it's a HI-PERF ratio.
If it's @3 turns or less it's a SMOG ratio.

With HI-PERF ratios 3-1/4 turns or more:
Install springs shown for Diesel in step 7.

With smog ratios @ 3 turns or less:
Adjusts springs so that lockup and 4th won't be later than most customers desire. Here's How:

With Normal Converter Clutch Valve: Cut 1/2 of the end coil off both ends of the RED spring as shown in picture. Or measure the free length of the spring and grind both ends to make spring .035 to .045 shorter.

With Long Stem Converter Clutch Valve: Don't use long stem type valve if you can avoid it. Rob a Normal type valve and bushing from another VB if possible. If you must use Long Stem type cut 4 1/2 coils off WHITE spring and install BROWN and WHITE spring.

With long stem valve, the job will work better if you retain the electrical UNlocking feature. This means if the electrical is working and the long stem valve is used, don't install a checkball in the solenoid.

With 1st design 3-4 Shift Valve: Use smaller diameter of the two unpainted springs furnished in small plastic bag.

With 2nd design 3-4 Shift Valve: Use larger diameter of the two unpainted springs furnished in small plastic bag.

Use snub nose dike

Shortening coil spring

Cut wire from the end. Don't cut between coils.

Some TWO WHEEL DRIVE cars and trucks with V6 or V8 may have factory towing package (or lower gears may have been installed). This means the vehicle has 3:22 to 4:11 axle ratio instead of 2:73 or 3:08 which is normally installed in 2WD vehicles.
This can cause lockup and 3-4 shift to be early. If you get this complant, check the axle ratio. If it's 3:22 to 4:11, install the springs in step seven shown for diesel.

Auxiliary valve body---87up

CHECKBALL

Fwd clutch accumulator

Forward Accm piston: Install a seal furnished that fits the groove correctly and installs in bore snugly.

INTERCHANGE
82-87 VB's interchange.
87-88 cases fit only 87up.
88 VB and plate fit only fit each other.
With the correct electrical connections, entire units interchange all years.

Mr Shift®

(OVER)

offer a range of separator-plate hole sizes. It is best to be on the conservative side to start out with. Many things can affect shift performance; such as engine RPM, input torque, and torque-converter efficiency. It's easier to go back in and open things up, than to start out with the largest separator-plate hole sizes in the first place.

Some shift kits will require drilling holes in the separator plate. They may not have the needed drill bits in the shift kit. Follow the size recommendations exactly, and make sure to check twice and drill once. If the wrong hole is drilled, don't panic, you can often reduce the size of the hole by inserting a small cotter pin into the hole and bending over and clipping the ends.

Accumulators

I do *not* recommend disabling accumulators. Accumulators are designed to provide some "cushion" to the shift. An accumulator is nothing more than a piston and seal trapped in a bore. A spring will be used behind the piston.

When hydraulic fluid pushes on the face of the piston, it will have to compress the spring behind the piston, in conjunction with applying a

Accumulators are used to control shift function. They provide a "cushion" for the shift by controlling oil-flow delivery to the clutch packs or servo. The oil flowing to the servo or clutch pack must compress the accumulator spring, while at the same time applying the servo or clutch-pack apply piston. The tension of the spring under the accumulator will determine how long it takes to fully compress. This basically "softens" the shift somewhat. Some shift kits recommend disabling accumulators, or blocking oil flow to them. This can lead to extremely quick and firm shifts, and apply considerable "shock" to the hard parts in the transmission.

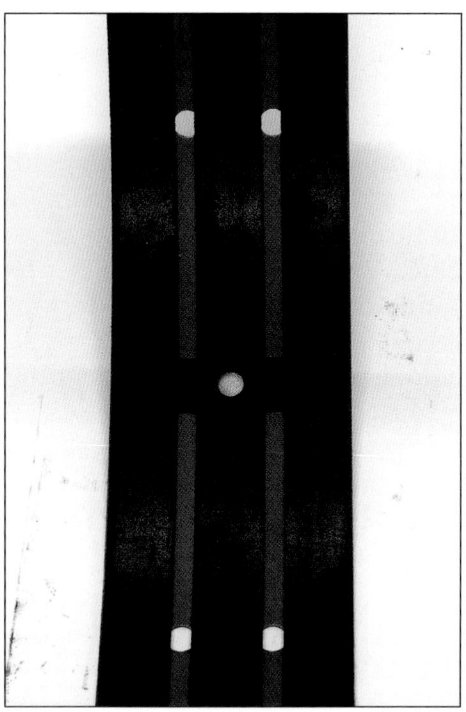

A well-cured band will be very dark, even black in appearance. This is considered normal and does not necessary mean that the band has failed or wasn't working properly.

servo or clutch-pack apply piston. The size of the piston and tension of the spring behind the piston will affect shift "feel," as well as how long it takes to complete the shift. Some transmission builders will turn pistons and springs over, block hydraulic fluid flow to them, disable them, or leave out the springs behind them. This will cause direct application of the apply piston when the transmission makes a shift. The shift will be shorter, or happen sooner, and it will also be firmer. This can affect shift timing, and may "shock" the hard parts, in contrast to having smooth application of the band or clutch pack.

The band has a lining on it, and the clutch packs use steel and friction plates. These parts are considered sacrificial, or designed to wear out and save the hard parts. Modern friction materials are well made, and will last a long time. The lining on the frictions and band will "cure" shortly after they are placed in service—sort of like the piston rings in an engine seating in. It is recommended that the transmission not be placed under heavy load for a few miles when first placed in service. This gives the band a chance to cure to the drum, and the steel and friction plates in the clutch packs a chance to wear in. You may even notice a change in shift performance as this happens. It is not uncommon for the 1-2 shift to be rather harsh or firm initially, then quickly settle in to a more smooth engagement. This is due to the band curing to the hard steel drum that it applies to. Many bands, when removed from high-mileage transmissions, will appear dark, or even black. This is actually a normal condition, and shows the results of a well-cured band.

Installing a shift kit requires patience and attention to detail. Several valves may need to be removed from the valve body. Study the pictures in the instructions carefully. The shift kit will include replacement springs that are color coded for identification. Some kits will add springs where before there weren't any. They may also contain new valves, as a common problem with early units was the TV valve sticking in the valve body, causing rough, erratic problems with shift performance.

Most shift kits will come with one or more plastic bags containing groups of springs, sometimes combined with other components. The contents of each bag should be kept together during the shift-kit installation process. When the bags are opened, a couple of small plastic food-storage containers make a great way to keep the components separated.

Prior to installing your shift kit, the valve body should be thoroughly cleaned and free of oil and grease. A large cookie sheet makes a great place to set the valve body during the process. As valves and springs are removed, they can be placed on the cookie sheet to keep them from ending up on the floor. Before starting your shift-kit installation, take a very small flat-tip screwdriver and test the operation of the various valves in the valve body. Locate and identify the valves that appear to be stuck. Shift kits do not usually require removing all the valves from the valve body, but you want to make sure that all the valves are operating correctly. Once the shift-kit installation is complete, remove and clean any valves that were not working correctly if they were not identified in the shift-kit instructions for removal or modification.

At first glance, the valve body looks complicated. To keep things simple only remove one valve at a time during the installation of the shift kit. Pay close attention to the valve's orientation, and which side the springs were on. It's pretty easy to get confused, and often the pictures in the shift kits are not all that

Shift kits contain a lot of parts. Some of them are extremely small. Very carefully open all the bags and keep the contents separated, as they are usually grouped together for convenience.

Clean the valve body thoroughly and place it on a large pan or cookie sheet. Make sure the pan is spotlessly clean, as any dirt or debris that may find its way into the valve body can have disastrous results when the transmission is placed in service.

Some shift kits come with a special tool to remove the small roll pins that retain the various valves in the transmission. Some of the pins are pushed into blind holes, and can be very difficult to remove.

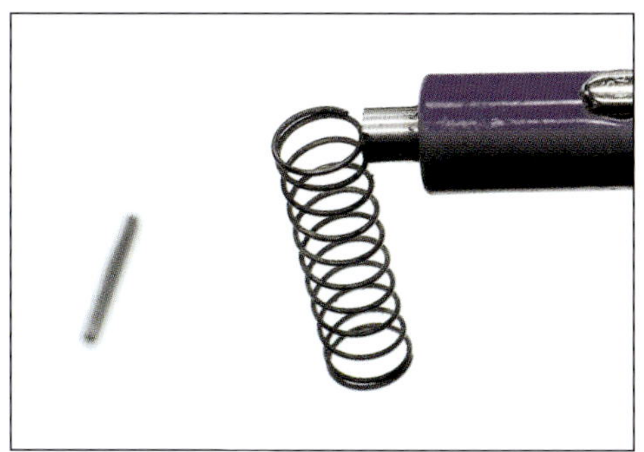

A small magnet or magnetic screwdriver can be useful to remove small springs and valves from the valve body.

good. 4L60s use small roll pins to retain the valves; there are clips to retain the electronic shift valves in the 4L60E models. To remove the small roll pins, some kits will include a custom tool. You can also fabricate your own tool from an old piece of flat spring steel. When your tool is inserted into the roll pin, turning it clockwise will facilitate removing the roll pin. On occasion the valve may stick. A small scribe or small screwdriver may be needed to put some additional pressure behind the valve to push it out. A small magnet may also be useful to pull some valves out of their bores. Use caution when removing any valves, as they may have quite a bit of spring pressure on them, and can be easily lost.

The springs provided in the shift kit will be color coded, and close in diameter and length to the springs being replaced. Some kits also offer options for springs based on the intended use of the vehicle, engine power output, etc. They may also provide a variety of springs to control shift firmness, or vary shift timing.

The TV, or throttle valve, has been a trouble spot for the 4L60 transmission since its introduction. Some aftermarket shift kits will supply a new valve, which uses an internal and external spring to help keep it from sticking.

All 4L60s prior to the electronically shifted models used a TV cable and governor to control all up and down shift points. The TV cable tells the transmission the throttle position of the carburetor or throttle body. The governor provides a vehicle speed reference, and the valve body provides all upshifts and downshifts accordingly. The TV cables are adjustable to provide the correct amount of movement to the TV valve, based on the throttle position of the carburetor or throttle body. Aftermarket adjustable cables are also available and make retrofitting a

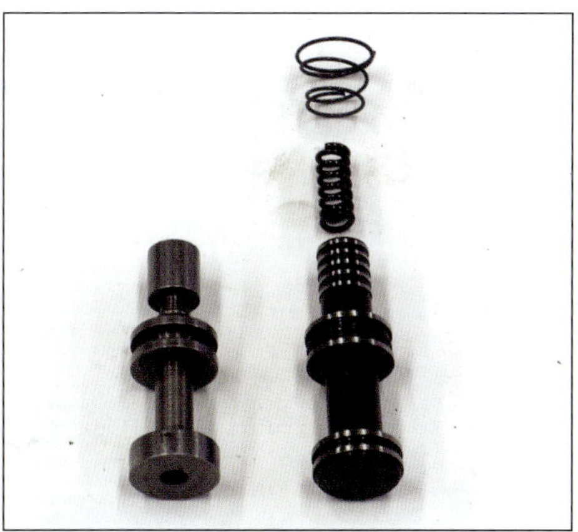

The components of the throttle valve are shown. The TV sleeve, plunger, and throttle valve let the transmission know the throttle position. The governor provides a vehicle-speed reference. There is no vacuum modulator used in the 4L60 transmission. The factory TV valves have always been a problem area, and are responsible for a high percentage of the 2-4-band and 3-4-clutch failures. The factory throttle valves can stick inside the bore in the valve body. Notice how the aftermarket TV valve is modified for less surface area in contact with the bore, and uses springs to help keep it from sticking. These valves are available separately from shift kits, and are highly recommended for all rebuilds.

4L60 into a non-factory application much easier. They are adjustable for total length of the cable, in addition to being adjustable for correct transmission function.

Most 4L60s would not allow high-speed cruising at heavy throttle positions in fourth gear or overdrive. At any throttle position greater than about two-thirds, the transmission will automatically shift from fourth to third, and remain in third until the throttle position is reduced. The Corvette and a few other special high-performance applications use a

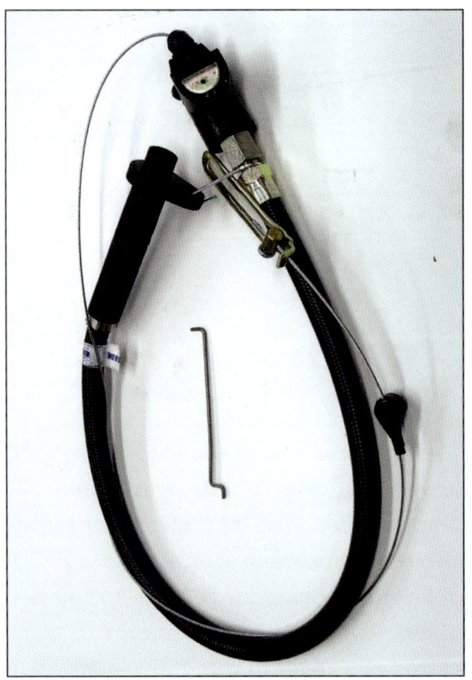

The 4L60 transmissions require a cable to operate the throttle valve in the valve body. This provides a reference signal to the transmission to control all upshifts and downshifts, based on vehicle speed. Note: TV-cable adjustment is critical to correct transmission function. If the cable is not providing enough movement of the TV valve, transmission shifts will be too early and "soft," and can result in transmission failure, as the line pressure may be too low for sufficient clutch-pack or band application. The vehicle-speed signal comes from the governor, which is driven by the transmission output shaft. All TV cables are adjustable at the cable end to provide the correct relationship between the throttle opening and TV-valve position. Aftermarket TV cables are available and make retrofitting a 4L60 transmission into a non-stock application much easier. The cables are not only adjustable for TV position, but for cable length as well. They also come with several different ends to make them easier to hook up to the carburetor or throttle body.

Most 4L60 transmissions will not upshift from third to fourth above about two-thirds throttle. Installing the Corvette 3-4 upshift sleeve over the TV valve will provide heavy- and full-throttle upshifts from third to fourth gear. This allows high-speed cruising at heavy throttle openings in fourth gear, which is not possible with 4L60 transmissions that do not use the Corvette TV sleeve.

modified sleeve over the TV valve, which allows fourth-gear operation at heavy throttle positions and high vehicle speeds. These TV sleeves are available aftermarket, and can be installed into any model to provide this function.

Corvette Servo

The Corvette transmissions also used a different servo to apply the band than other models. It has more surface area, which provides a firmer shift and more holding power for the band. The Corvette servo is recommended for all heavy-duty and high-performance applications. The aftermarket also offers even larger servos. I don't consider any servo larger than the Corvette model necessary; it has proved large enough to provide sufficient holding power for the band in high-performance applications. High-performance aftermarket bands are also available for the 4L60 transmissions. They offer special lining, and increased strength of the mounting area where the apply strut is attached. The factory band with the red lining has proven to be a very good part, and suitable for high-performance applications when combined with the Corvette servo assembly and sufficient line pressure to the servo.

The Corvette servo shown on the right has more surface area to provide greater holding power for the band. They are highly recommended for all rebuilds. The aftermarket has even larger servos available, but the Corvette servo is fine for all but the most serious high-performance applications.

The boost valve is located above the pressure-regulator valve in the oil pump. It is used to boost line pressure. Several different sizes were used. The larger boost valves may come in high-performance shift kits, and should be used according to the directions supplied with that kit. Installing a larger boost valve in an otherwise stock transmission may have negative results, as other items in the valve body are programmed for lower line pressures.

Boost Valves

The pressure-regulating valves also used a boost valve to control line pressure. Several different boost valves were used for various applications. The larger boost valves will provide firmer shifts and overall more aggressive transmission function. Different boost valves are available from the aftermarket. Some shift kits will refer to the different boost valves in their shift-kit instructions, and provide different changes for the different valves. Pay close attention to this part of the procedure to make sure the correct modifications coincide with the correct boost-valve size. I do not recommend that the builder simply go out and purchase and install the largest boost valve available.

Large Valve Problems

The larger valves can have a negative impact on shift performance, raising shift points and firming up shifts to a level that may not be acceptable to the driver. Large boost valves should only be installed if the shift-kit directions specifically state to do so, or the builder has considerable experience with a particular combination of parts that worked well with the larger boost valves.

Separator Plates

The 4L60 and 4L60E transmissions used a steel separator plate and steel check balls. The check balls seal against the plate to control the direction of fluid flow. Some units will have experienced minor wear on the plate, caused by many thousands of shifts over the life of the transmission. It is not uncommon to see the steel balls stuck, or even pushed clear through the steel plate. If the wear is minor, and the steel balls still show they are able to seal, the separator plate can be placed back in service. If heavily worn, the plate must be replaced. Another option is to repair the plate. Check-ball repair kits are available and easy to install. Some kits will recommend leaving out one or more check balls. Make sure before replacing or repairing the separator plate that the hole in question is indeed going to be used with the new shift kit.

Torque Converter Clutch

The torque converter used by these transmissions is equipped with a clutch. Its purpose and function is

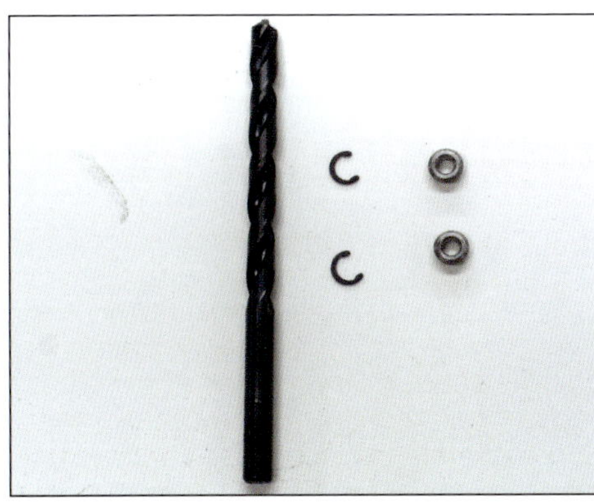

The steel check balls used in the case and valve body can damage the separator plate. In lieu of replacing the plate, you can repair the damaged areas by installing a new seat. Simply drill the plate with the bit provided, install a new seat so the new seat faces the check ball, and snap on the retaining clip.

The torque-converter clutch is located inside the torque converter. The part shown is a large apply piston with friction lining molded to it. Oil pressure coming up through the input shaft pushes the apply piston forward. This forces the friction lining against the inside of the torque-converter front drive cover. Since the apply piston is splined internally to the turbine, which drives the input shaft, the torque converter ceases all torque multiplication. It is basically "locked up," and provides a direct drive between the engine and the transmission.

An electric solenoid is mounted in the transmission oil pump. A solenoid is nothing more than an electrically operated switch. When voltage is applied to the solenoid, it provides high-pressure oil flow to the input shaft. The oil flows under pressure inside the converter to push the TCC apply piston forward, applying the clutch.

outlined in Chapter 5. Basically, by using hydraulic fluid, a clutch inside the torque converter is applied to cease all torque multiplication, and provide a solid 1:1 power-transfer ratio between the engine and the transmission. When the TCC (torque converter clutch) is applied, the transmission basically feels like it just made a gear change, or shift. This reduces the amount of heat created inside the converter. It also helps improve fuel economy, by reducing engine RPM and transferring all the engine power directly to the transmission.

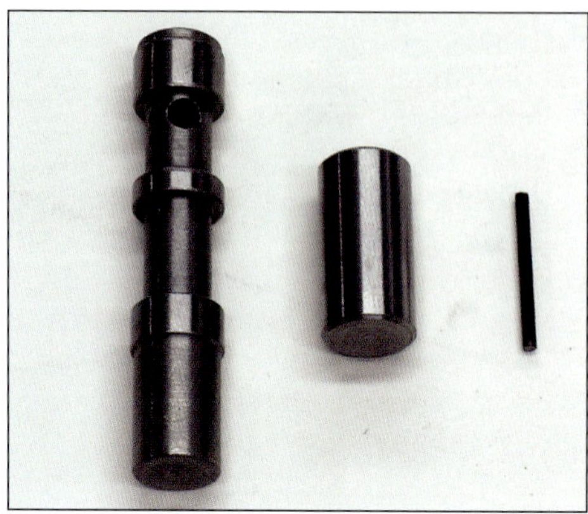

If you are converting to a non-lock-up torque converter, a special valve is used in the oil pump to replace the lock-up valve. The check ball is also removed from the front of the input shaft. This redirects fluid flow through the torque converter and transmission to make sure they work correctly with the non-lock-up converter.

The factory used an electrically activated solenoid to provide TCC operation. Depending on the application the transmission was used in, this could happen as early as second gear, and continue through third and fourth (OD). Some units used the TCC only in third and fourth, some in fourth only.

In factory applications, the TCC is not applied in low gear. It is also not applied when the vehicle is

Several aftermarket kits are available to provide correct TCC function. The voltage to the TCC solenoid is routed through a vacuum switch, and then grounded on a fourth-gear pressure switch. This will only allow TCC engagement in fourth gear, at light to moderate throttle positions. Since the vacuum switch is hooked up to ported vacuum, the TCC will not apply when idling, coasting, or at heavy- and full-throttle openings. Some kits will also route the voltage through the brake-pedal switch as a fail-safe to make sure the TCC can not apply when the vehicle is stopped, which would immediately shut down the engine. A toggle switch can also be used in the supply voltage wire to the transmission, for manual control of the TCC if needed.

coasting. Computerized vehicles use a reference signal from the TPS (throttle position sensor) to apply the TCC when the vehicle is accelerating or cruising at a steady speed. The TCC is also not applied at heavy and full throttle. Disengaging the TCC during coasting and heavy or full throttle application allows for torque multiplication, and avoids overloading the TCC, or lugging the engine. At idle in low gear the TCC must not apply or the engine would stall.

For stock applications, I recommend re-installing the stock wiring harness, which will have the TCC work as it was intended by the factory. For retrofitting or high-performance applications, the TCC works best if only applied in fourth gear or OD (overdrive), for light-throttle cruising. If the transmission is being installed in a high-performance vehicle you may choose not to run a TCC at all. Aftermarket high-performance torque converters are available without a TCC. A non-lock-up valve must be installed with a non-lock-up converter, and the check ball and capsule removed from the front of the input shaft.

For retrofitting, several aftermarket kits are available to provide correct TCC operation. In vehicles with a carburetor, a vacuum switch is installed and hooked to a ported source. A ported vacuum source is located above the throttle plates, and will only provide vacuum to the switch at light throttle. Any coasting, idling, or heavy-to-wide-open-throttle reduces the vacuum to near zero. Since the vacuum switch is normally "open," it will cut power to the TCC during these situations. The TCC will only operate when the throttle position is low, and the engine load is light. The voltage from the vacuum switch is routed through the TCC solenoid, and grounded on a fourth-gear pressure switch. The fourth-gear pressure switch is also normally "open," and only closes to provide a ground for the solenoid when the transmission is in fourth gear.

Some of these kits also include a switch to run in line, so the voltage to the TCC solenoid can be turned on or off when desired. They may also run the voltage through a brake-pedal switch, to ensure that the TCC disengages when the vehicle's brakes are applied or it comes to a stop. Another common way to set up the TCC in older vehicles is to run the voltage directly to the TCC solenoid, then on to a fourth-gear pressure switch. This will only allow TCC operation in fourth gear. The

Temperature Switch

Some models used a temperature switch in the wiring harness that applied the TCC solenoid.

Some transmissions use a temperature switch to prevent TCC application until the transmission is fully warmed up. These switches can fail, and cause a loss of TCC operation. They should always be checked or replaced during rebuilding.

This prevents TCC operation until the transmission reaches operating temperature. These switches were notorious for going bad, which lead to loss of TCC operation. This could lead to transmission overheating, and failure, due to excessive heat produced by internal slippage inside the torque converter, when the vehicle is operated in high gear for long periods of time. It is recommended to replace the temperature switch for all rebuilds. For retrofitting and high-performance applications, the temperature switch is not needed. An easy way to disable the temperature switch is to make a jumper wire to go across both terminals, or carefully solder a small jumper wire between the terminals and hook the switch up with the stock wiring harness.

A jumper wire can be made up to bypass the temperature switch, or the wires can be soldered together and have heat-shrink tubing melted over them. There are no negatives from doing so that I have been able to determine. Many 4L60 transmissions didn't use a temperature switch at all.

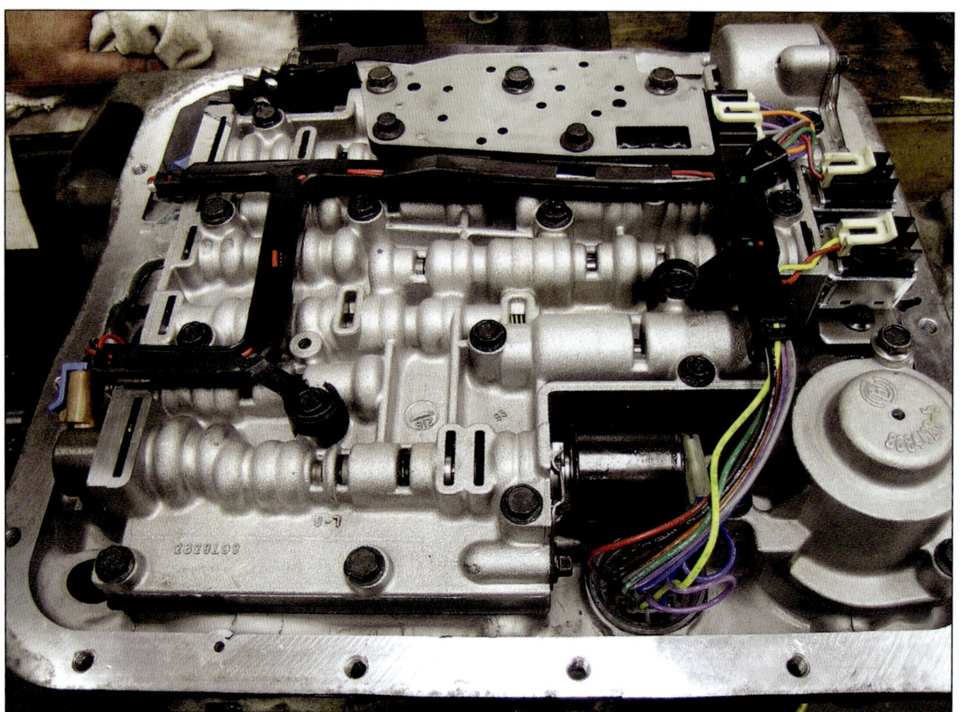

A new wiring harness should be included with any 4L60E rebuild. This ensures that you will not have any wiring troubles inside the transmission pan.

I recommend replacing all of the electronics when rebuilding a 4L60E transmission. Service packages are available that contain all of the shift switches, a pressure-control switch, and a new TCC solenoid. Make sure to install a new wiring harness; this adds some cost to the rebuild, but it's well worth the additional expense.

downside of not using a vacuum switch is that the TCC will always be engaged in fourth gear, regardless of engine load or throttle position.

Shift kits are also available for the 4L60E transmissions. Even though they are ECM controlled for all shifts, shift firmness can be improved. When rebuilding a 4L60E transmission, it is highly recommended to replace the wiring harness and all of the electronic components.

Complete service packages are available. Even though they increase the cost of the rebuild, they ensure that the electronic portion of the transmission will work correctly when it is placed in service.

Applying voltage to the terminals with jumper leads from a 12-volt battery can check the factory shift switches and pressure-regulating switch. Some builders perform this check as standard procedure during an overhaul of the 4L60E transmission. An audible "click" can be heard as the solenoids operate when the voltage and ground are applied to the terminals. This means that the solenoid is operating, but does not necessarily mean that the internals of the switch are in good working order. It is recommended to replace all the electronic components, especially if the transmission you are working on was giving you troubles and you don't find anything wrong in the clutch packs or with the servo and band. The probability at this point would be pretty high that the unit was experiencing electronic-component troubles. The moderate additional cost to replace all of the electronics far outweighs the chances that the unit may not work properly, and you would have to go back inside and change some or all of the components anyhow.

Torque Converters

Torque converters are fascinating. They are bolted to the engine and provide a fluid coupling to the transmission. We often take torque converters for granted, but their implementation was a tremendous breakthrough in the development of modern automatic transmissions. Various techniques for coupling the engine to the rest of the drivetrain by electric and vacuum-operated clutches, fluid-drive mechanisms, and Henry Ford's foot-actuated planetary drives in his Model Ts have been tried. All worked to some degree, but all had disadvantages. Modern torque converters are extremely efficient, and even include hydraulically operated internal clutches that can be applied to cease all torque multiplication, and provide a solid mechanical drive to the transmission. These started showing up in the late 1970s, as ever-tightening emissions standards demanded the least amount of pollutants exiting the tailpipes of production vehicles. The engineers found that by adding a clutch to the torque

The 4L60 and 4L60E transmissions used a three-element torque converter with the addition of a torque-converter clutch. Obtaining a new or rebuilt torque converter is highly recommended for all rebuilt transmissions. It is nearly impossible to correctly clean and flush a used converter, and there are several items inside the converter that can wear out.

converter, they could reduce engine RPM even further when the vehicle was at speed. They could lock and unlock the torque-converter clutch when needed to provide torque multiplication for improved vehicle acceleration, such as passing maneuvers, then apply the converter clutch for maximum power transfer and efficiency for light-throttle operation at highway speeds.

History of Torque Converters

The first use of hydraulic coupling to connect a power plant to a load occurred in the early 1900s, when a German engineer coupled a ship turbine to the propeller via a fluid drive device. The same engineer also devised a coupling with an enclosed reaction unit to increase torque. This torque-improving device was the first torque converter in use and, since it incorporated the stator (reaction member) to multiply torque, it formed the basic design for all modern torque converters.

The first automotive torque converter was tested in the 1920s in Germany, and torque converters were used in railcars in the 1930s. Later, a truck was produced in Sweden in the 1930s with a torque converter. The first torque converter used by GM was installed in a 1949 Buick Dynaflow automatic transmission, and the first Pontiac transmission to be so equipped was the 1961 3-speed Roto Hydra-Matic. The earlier 4-speed Hydra-Matic utilized a fluid coupling, which is similar to a converter but does not utilize the third element to multiply torque.

The 1939 Chrysler Imperial was the first car to use a fluid coupling. Ford initially used a fluid coupling in 1942 that had been developed by BorgWarner and was used in some models of the 1942 Lincoln and Mercury cars. GM initially used a fluid coupling in a 1940 Oldsmobile, and it was incorporated into the 1941 Cadillac. While the fluid coupling was similar in operation for each manufacturer, the transmission designs and operation varied widely. They provided relatively good efficiency when coupled, but they generally did not provide the desired standing-start acceleration. The GM 4-speed Hydra-Matic solved this problem by incorporating a very low first gear (3.81 to 3.97, depending on the model) in conjunction with the fluid coupling to improve acceleration, and this combination was used from 1940 to 1964 in Oldsmobiles, Cadillacs, and Pontiacs.

Fluid Couplings

The first true American automobile torque-converter transmission was designed and introduced by Buick in 1948 as the Dynoflow—it was an available option on the Roadmaster model. Buick continued to use the Dynaflow name for years, but the later converters and transmissions were highly modified as Buick attempted to resolve the leisurely acceleration while retaining the very smooth "shiftless" feel.

The 1949 Packard was next with a true torque-converter transmission, called the Ultramatic. Ford, in conjunction with BorgWarner, released their first torque converter-equipped transmission in 1950. Studebaker also used a version of the BorgWarner unit, and it became an option in 1950. Chevrolet released the Powerglide with a torque converter. It was loosely based on the Buick Dynaflow, but was simplified with only two speeds and a simpler converter design.

Ford released the Fordomatic and Mercomatic torque-converter transmissions in 1951. They incorporated three speeds in addition to the initial torque multiplication of the torque converter. GM continued to rely on the 4-speed, fluid-coupled Hydra-Matic for Olds, Pontiac, and Cadillac cars. It went through a major redesign in 1956, which made it much smoother shifting. However, the competitors had all switched to torque converters, and these provided smoother operation and a more performance-oriented feel. So the GM Hydra-Matic Division made its first tentative step with torque converters in the Roto Hydra-Matic in 1963, and these were used in certain models of both Oldsmobile and Pontiac.

The first modern GM automatic was released in 1965 as the Turbo Hydromatic in the Oldsmobile, Pontiac, and Cadillac cars, and it incorporated a three-element torque converter, three forward gears, and overrunning clutches that allowed the next higher gear to pick up the load from the preceding gear. The entire line of current GM transmissions has descended from the TH400. Chevrolet developed a 3-speed automatic called the Turboglide. It resembled the Buick Dynaflow.

Chrysler introduced what was then the most modern and efficient automatic transmission with its Torqueflite. It incorporated a three-element torque converter and three separate gears. It proved to be the prototype of most automatics for many years.

All of the torque-converter transmissions mentioned were being continuously improved, and some were renamed.

How It Works

What is the difference between a fluid coupling and a torque converter, and how do they actually transfer power? I have seen depictions of power flow through a fluid coupling as two ordinary household cooling fans facing each other. One fan is powered up, and the air it blows causes the non-powered fan to turn. The fluid coupling operates similarly to the fan example, except that ATF (automatic transmission fluid), rather than air, is the medium used to transfer power. The ATF for the fluid coupling (and torque converters) is furnished by the automatic-transmission gear-type oil pump. Both halves of a fluid coupling are constructed identically with flat-type vanes.

The TH400 converter shown is from a 1969 Pontiac transmission. Unlike the 4L60 torque converters, no clutch was used inside the unit.

The torque converter incorporates one major change from the fluid coupling: a third element (the stator) is designed into the unit. The stator consists of a finned element that fits between the driving member (impeller) and the driven member (turbine), and it is mounted via a one-way clutch to the turbine. In addition, the vanes of the impeller and turbine are curved, and are oriented differently in the two units. The curved vane construction allows the ATF to change directions rather gradually as it passes between the impeller and the turbine. This gradual change of direction imparts more force to the turbine as the oil strikes it.

Torque Converter Operation

A torque converter has the impeller connected to the engine, while the turbine is connected to the mechanical portion of the transmission. Upon engine startup, the transmission oil pump pressurizes the converter with ATF. The impeller throws the ATF into bucket-like receptacles of the turbine and generates some pressure on the turbine in the same direction as the impeller is turning. After striking the turbine, the ATF is deflected back toward the impeller. As the engine speed increases, additional ATF velocity develops due to impeller action, and without a stator installed, the ATF would be reflected back from the turbine to the impeller in a direction that impedes the impeller operation. With a stator installed, the stator vanes redirect the returning ATF so that it strikes the impeller elements in the correct direction.

At the same time, the stator adds the energy from the returning ATF to the turbine shaft. This energy, added to the original energy transferred from the impeller to the turbine, is what causes the "torque multiplication" in a converter at low RPM. In a typical stock converter it is about a 2:1 multiplication factor. As the RPM increases, the angle of the returning oil from the turbine changes and, at some point, the stator fins begin to impede the flow of ATF. The one-way (roller) clutch in the stator allows the stator to begin to turn on the shaft so as not to affect the ATF flow. At that point, the converter is "coupled," and the converter now operates at an approximate 1:1 ratio.

The stock TH400 torque converter, for example, multiples torque 2:1 at low RPM so that a moderate-ratio first gear can be used. The torque-converter multiplication and the 2.48 gear give a 5:1 stall ratio, and this combination provides excellent acceleration from a stop. Second gear is 1.48:1, and third is 1:1 (direct drive), so the steps between each gear are relatively small, which provides efficient and smooth shifts. Some torque multiplication also occurs in second and third gears at lower RPM.

The front drive cover is a heavy-duty shell that bolts to the engine's flywheel or flex plate.

To eliminate torque multiplication at higher vehicle speeds, a clutch was added to the torque converter on the 700-R4 and 4L60 transmissions. This provided a direct 1:1 drive between the engine's flywheel and the transmission's input shaft. Adding a clutch to the torque converter not only provided a direct coupling between the engine and transmission, it reduced heat production, lowered engine RPM, and increased the effective power transfer to the rear wheels. When driving a vehicle equipped with a 4L60 transmission and torque-converter clutch, the application of the TCC feels much like an additional shift. If the vehicle is equipped with an engine tachometer, the driver will notice the engine RPM decreases slightly. If a heavy load is placed on the engine, requiring heavy throttle position, the TCC will unlock and provide torque multiplication to take some load off the engine. This will also allow it to more effectively transfer the additional power required to increase the vehicle speed, or maintain it on a steep grade, for example. The unlocking of the TCC may also coincide with a shift to a lower gear. Exactly how this is accomplished is explained in previous chapters. Basically, the TCC is only employed for light load and light throttle application, and is disengaged for heavy- and full-throttle positions and when coasting.

To show how a modern 4L60 converter works, I have obtained a sample from Continental Torque Converters. The various internal components are shown, with a brief description of their roles in torque-converter function.

Front Drive Cover

The front drive cover is a large, heavy-duty metal housing that is bolted directly to the engine's flywheel.

It turns with the engine's crankshaft to directly transmit all engine power to the transmission, through the internal components of the torque converter. Early 4L60 torque converters used round pads for the mounting bolts, which were welded directly to the front drive cover. Later units used wider mounting pads for the bolts, which were less prone to leaking at the welds and provided a stronger mounting surface.

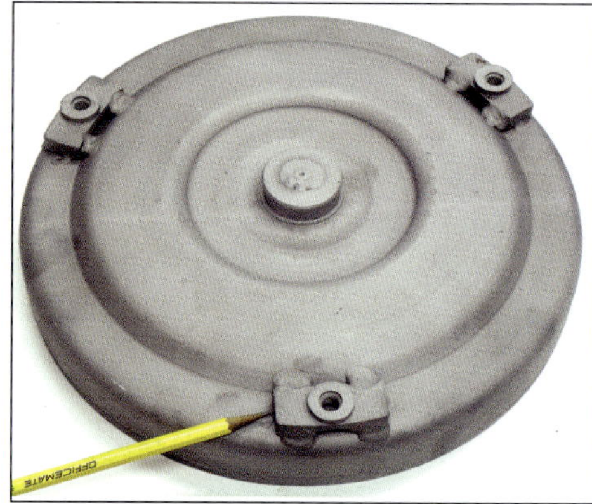

The front drive cover mounting pads are shown here. Early units used round pads with less surface area welded to the drive cover. The welds would occasionally fail, so the larger mounting pads were added to increase durability.

A phenolic spacer is used in the front of the torque converter. The spacer effectively seals the input shaft O-ring to keep fluid pressure from bleeding off when the torque-converter clutch is applied.

An O-ring is used on the outer portion of the input shaft to seal against the phenolic spacer inside the torque converter. A check ball and capsule are also installed into the end of the input shaft to control oil flow to the torque-converter clutch.

An O-ring seals the outer portion of the phenolic spacer against the TCC apply piston.

Carbon Phenolic Spacer

A carbon phenolic spacer is installed just behind the front cover.

It is used to seal up the inner O-ring on the turbine shaft.

The spacer has an outer O-ring that seals inside the TCC apply piston, ensuring that all oil coming up through the turbine shaft is used to apply the TCC.

Torque Converter Pump

The torque-converter pump, or impeller, is the back outer shell of the torque converter. It contains the pump drive, which is inserted into the transmission and drives the transmission oil pump.

Inside the housing is a series of vanes. Since the torque-converter pump is welded to the front drive cover, the vanes always spin at engine speed. They work like fan blades, constantly moving oil out and away from them.

The back half of the torque converter uses a notched hub, which engages and drives the transmission oil pump. When installing the torque converter into the transmission, you must make sure that the notches are fully engaged into the oil pump before installing the bell-housing-to-engine bolts. If the hub is not engaged, tightening the bolts will break the oil pump, and could damage the torque converter.

The oil pump uses a series of vanes. Since the oil pump is welded to the front cover, it is driven directly by the engine's crankshaft, and is always moving oil. The amount of oil moved by the vanes is directly proportional to engine speed.

The torque converter turbine is splined directly to the transmission input shaft. It also uses vanes similar in appearance to those used by the oil pump. The oil pump moves oil into the turbine vanes, where they react to the oil flow and turn it into mechanical energy.

The stator assembly is splined directly to the stator splines on the transmission. The vanes in the stator are used to redirect some of the oil flow from the oil pump, back to the turbine, to increase its efficiency.

The transmission stator splines are fixed, or stationary, in the transmission oil pump. They spline into the torque-converter stator, and allow the one-way roller clutch to hold to improve torque-converter function.

The oil is routed through the other components in the torque converter to turn the input shaft in the transmission.

Turbine

The turbine is located directly in front of the torque-converter pump, inside the torque converter.

It receives the oil flowing from the pump, and converts it into mechanical energy. The turbine is splined directly to the transmission's input shaft. It contains a series of vanes, much like the torque-converter pump. The number of vanes found on the pump and turbine—and their size, length, and angle—determine the overall efficiency of the torque converter.

Stator

The stator is located between the torque-converter pump and the turbine. It is a key player in torque-converter efficiency.

A one-way roller sprag, or clutch, is used in the stator assembly. The one-way clutch is applied at low engine and vehicle speeds, redirecting fluid back to the turbine. This greatly increases torque-converter efficiency, as the oil flowing away from the turbine would otherwise be lost energy.

The apply piston for the torque-converter clutch, or TCC, has a lot of surface area. This provides sufficient holding power when high-pressure oil is applied to the piston to hold it against the torque-converter front cover.

The stator contains a roller one-way clutch, similar to what is used inside the transmission for the low/reverse clutch.

The inside splined portion of the one-way clutch is engaged in the front of the transmission's stator shaft.

At low engine speeds, the one-way clutch is on and holding. This causes the oil flow from the torque-converter pump to route through the stator fins, adding backpressure to the turbine. The result is improved efficiency as the engine speed increases, and improved torque multiplication. Eventually the torque-converter pump and the turbine reach approximately the same speed and the one-way clutch releases.

Friction material is added to the front of the apply piston to help it hold firmly when applied.

The large splines on the apply piston engage the turbine. When the piston is applied, it will turn at the same speed as the front cover. This effectively couples the engine's flywheel to the transmission's input shaft. When applied, all torque multiplication between the oil pump, stator, and turbine ceases, and all of the engine's power is applied directly to the transmission's input shaft.

Large springs are added to the apply piston to reduce "shudder" and provide smooth engagement of the TCC.

Piston Dampener Assembly

The torque converters used in 4L60 transmissions contain a TCC, or torque-converter clutch.

A large apply piston, or piston dampener assembly, contains friction material that is forced against the backside of the front drive cover.

The piston dampener assembly has internal splines that are meshed with splines found on the back of the turbine.

Since the turbine is splined directly to the transmission's input shaft, it will cease torque multiplication when the piston dampener assembly is applied. The large springs are used to smooth the application of the clutch.

Slippage vs. Torque vs. Vehicle Weight

If a typical converter-equipped vehicle is held stationary by the brakes, the engine started, the transmission placed in Drive, and the throttle opened, the engine will accelerate to some RPM level. This RPM point is called the stall RPM, and it is determined by two factors: the power (torque) that the engine can deliver at that RPM, and the converter slippage. If a 350-ci engine can stall a given converter to 1,800 rpm, a 472-ci engine would stall the same converter several hundred RPM higher due to the increased torque of the 472 at 1,800 rpm. What about the load the converter sees? If the typical vehicle described above (with either a 350 or 472) is driven normally, it will move out briskly from a stop with minimum converter slippage. However, if a 5,000-lb trailer is connected to the vehicle, increased power will be required to move the vehicle, and the converter will slip to a higher RPM with either engine before the vehicle begins to move. This exercise illustrates that converters are sensitive to both power and the load imposed upon them. The stall RPM does not change with load because the drivetrain is locked when the stall RPM is determined. However, the converter coupling is sensitive to load. Thus, there can be no accurate description of the stall RPM and relative slippage of a converter unless both the low RPM engine torque and the load (vehicle weight) are known.

Torque Converter Characteristics

Several general terms are frequently associated with torque converters. The following is a brief description of several of the terms I frequently hear, or see posted when browsing through catalogs listing various types and sizes of high-performance converters available.

Converter Stall RPM: The engine RPM that a given engine will reach at full throttle with the drivetrain locked. Holding the brakes and applying the throttle while the vehicle is in gear can determine this RPM. If a tachometer is available, you can see at what RPM the tires begin to spin and overcome the resistance placed on them by the brakes.

The use of a high-performance or high-stall-speed torque converter can dramatically improve starting-line performance. The car in the near lane is the author's daily driven street car, which runs 11-second quarter-mile times in full street trim. The transmission is equipped with a custom-built aftermarket torque converter supplied by Continental Torque Converters. It is designed to be very efficient for normal driving. At the track the converter stalls at approximately 3,500 rpm, for excellent drag-strip runs. The converter is locked nearly solid above the stall speed, and has been in service for many years, without any additional transmission cooling required.

Converter Flash RPM: The engine RPM that a given engine will reach at full throttle at the point the vehicle begins to move with no brake application. Both stall and flash must be checked from idle speed. Flash stall may be more difficult to determine exactly, unless the vehicle has sufficient traction so the tires do not spin when a quick full-throttle load is applied to the torque converter.

Converter Coupling Efficiency: The relative amount of slippage after the converter is "coupled." Coupling efficiency can also be difficult to determine exactly. One excellent way to measure a converter's coupling efficiency is at the drag strip. If you can determine the MPH that your vehicle crosses the finish line in high gear (1:1 ratio), and the engine RPM that you were running at that time, you can use a simple math formula to determine how many RPM the converter was slipping.

The physical size of stock converters will generally affect the coupling efficiency; the larger-diameter converters usually slip less than the smaller units. However, modifications to the converter's internal design can change both the stall speed and the coupling efficiency, regardless of size. Also, the angles and shapes of the fins in the impeller, turbine, and stator will have a major effect on both the coupling action and the stall speed of the converter.

In the earlier days of converters and hot rodding, the hot tip was to install a smaller converter, such as from the Chevrolet Vega, in place of the stock unit. This allowed the engine to reach a higher RPM before the converter began to transfer enough power to move the vehicle. While this did provide some advantages of low-speed acceleration, it also caused excessive slippage at higher speeds. The slippage destroyed top speed and gas mileage, and also generated a large amount of heat in the ATF. Such converter slippage will accelerate the failure rate of most converters.

Unfortunately, many of the speed-shop "universal converters" sold today are basically smaller converters with some minor construction features to enhance durability. Most are intended for the relatively low torque of a small-block Chevy. While they will provide higher stall, they may slip excessively when installed in heavier cars, with the high torque generated by most larger-displacement engines.

Selecting a Converter

As with most major components, the intended use is paramount when selecting a converter. A drag-race vehicle is usually lighter, has more radical drivetrain gearing, less concern for transmission/fluid overheating, no concern for fuel mileage, and normally has a higher-RPM-range engine with very little low-end torque. It's obvious that an optimum converter for such an application is far removed from a street or street/strip vehicle that is actually driven for normal transportation.

Coupled Efficency of a Torque Converter

By using the following formula, you can determine the coupled efficiency of your torque converter.

RPM = MPH x GEAR RATIO x 336 ÷ TIRE DIAMETER

Using my own vehicle as an example, I cross the finish line at 117 mph, at approximately 5,100 rpm. The vehicle uses 3.42 rear gears and 27-in-tall tires. By inserting your numbers into the formula, 117 mph times 3.42 times 336, divided by 27 equals 4,979 rpm.

Since I see right at 5,100 rpm at the end of the quarter-mile, the converter slippage is approximately 200 rpm, or about 2.4 percent. This is an example of a very efficient torque converter, considering the flash stall is approximately 3,500 rpm, and the load stall is right at 1,900 rpm. The converter was also custom built exactly for your application, by providing all of the engine, drivetrain, and vehicle specifications to the manufacturer, Continental Torque Converters in California.

Torque converters vary in diameter. Smaller torque converters are often used for high-performance or racing applications. The smaller-diameter converters can be set up to provide higher stall speeds and improved starting-line performance.

The typical stock engine will have a usable power range from idle to 5,000 to 5,500 rpm. As a stock converter will begin to transfer enough power to move the car at very low RPM, the usable RPM range is approximately 5,000. If the low-speed characteristics are modified to move the idle range up by longer-duration cams, excessively large-port heads, high-RPM manifolds, and/or large-tube headers, more power is usually lost at low RPM than is gained on the top end. The usable power range becomes noticeably smaller.

If a converter that will actually stall to 3,500 rpm is installed, the usable power range is reduced to a point that normal driving becomes difficult, although optimum quarter-mile acceleration may be achieved. In order to provide the best combination of acceleration, speed, and driveability, the converter should allow the engine to stall just to the beginning of the strong torque range. Any additional increase in stall RPM will begin to waste the good low-RPM torque range. Additionally, the higher stall is normally accompanied by greater slippage at higher speed, causing excess ATF heat, less MPH, and greater fuel consumption.

Another important factor of slippage is the effect on gear changes. At a shift point of 5,200 rpm, the engine will drop to 3,500 at the start of the next gear in a typical 3-speed automatic transmission. If the converter is not fully coupled at that shift RPM, a loss of acceleration may occur, and by the time the converter is coupled, it is almost time to shift again (or run out of RPM in high gear). A very loose converter may improve 60-ft and eighth-mile times for a lightweight race car, and might even help with quarter-mile times. However, a normal-RPM-range street car is likely to lose performance in the quarter-mile with such a converter, and the loose converter may not allow the car to run the full quarter-mile without hitting the redline.

Effects of Tight/Loose Converters

Because of the almost infinite number of combinations of engine components, gearing, and vehicle weights, and the variety of available converters, it is very difficult to conduct meaningful performance tests of specific converters. However, as converter technology improves, we are seeing more converters that can multiply starting-line torque, yet retain excellent coupling at higher RPM. And that tighter coupling minimizes loss of MPH at the track, as well as improving transmission oil cooling.

Aftermarket Converters

Aftermarket companies, such as Continental Torque Converters, employ a wide range of techniques to improve performance, including smaller converter size; different shapes and angles of fins on the pump, turbine, and stator; and different positioning of the various components. The techniques used are generally regarded as company secrets and are not willingly revealed. In addition to the changes for performance, there are a wide variety of modifications and additions made for converter strength and reliability.

What Should You Do For a Converter?

The overall performance of most stock cars with stock engines is usually best when using stock converters. The heavier cars with very high gearing (2.21 to 2.73) will respond well to slightly looser converters. Minor changes in camshafts that push the power range up in RPM may require a different converter.

As with any major component of the drivetrain, reliability, warranty, and performance of the converter must be considered along with its initial cost. If a significant change in engine power or RPM characteristics is incorporated, a custom-made converter should be considered. Contact the major suppliers or manufacturers of converters with your specific vehicle and engine specifications.

I have seen quarter-mile gains of as much as .4 seconds on moderately built street/strip cars with a change from stock to well-matched custom-type converters. Yet, at part throttle the quality converters drive and act similarly to a stock unit.

The 4L60 transmissions also have the advantage of being able to use a torque converter with a clutch, or TCC. This allows for more stall to be used, and you still have the benefits of being able to apply the TCC and lock up the torque converter to cease all torque multiplication at higher vehicle speeds in third and/or fourth gear. This doesn't mean that you can simply go out and buy (or have built) an extremely loose converter for your street car. Converters that lack good coupling efficiency at low engine RPM can be difficult to tolerate on a daily basis, and still produce a lot of heat during normal driving when the TCC is not applied. Torque-converter selection is often a compromise between a good stall ratio and efficient characteristics for street driving. Converters being made and sold today are better than ever, and with a well-built unit you can enjoy excellent starting-line performance combined with very good manners for everyday driving.

Quarter-Mile Driving Techniques

For quicker reaction times at the track, it may be necessary to raise the starting RPM some. As the good aftermarket converters tend to "hook" at higher RPM, the car will not move as briskly as stock-type units at light throttle. This in turn may cause traction problems. However, the launch has a major effect on the final elapsed time, and in order to best utilize the current quality converters, traction must be addressed, as well as the engine power range and final gearing.

Tips for Selecting a Converter

Keep the following points in mind when you choose a converter:

1. If your car is driven regularly on the street, it probably is not a race car, and race-car converters won't provide satisfactory overall performance.

2. Don't install a converter designed for a small-block into a car with a large-displacement or high-torque engine. Some companies state right in their ads "not for use with big-block engines." This statement doesn't mean that the converter is low quality and the additional torque from a strong-running big-block engine is going to kill it. It means that the low-speed coupling efficiency is designed more for engines that produce less torque. High-torque big-block engines, or even large-displacement small-block engines, should use converters closely matched to their power output at lower engine speeds.

3. Don't install a converter that is too loose with a street RPM engine. Otherwise, you'll run out of RPM much too early in the quarter-mile. Most vehicles are set up to go through the quarter-mile in high gear (1:1 ratio). Use the formula on page 97 to select the proper gearing for the vehicle if it is going to see a lot of time at the drag strip. Keep in mind that converter efficiency, once coupled, can greatly affect the engine RPM at the trap speed. We've seen loose converters slip nearly 1,000 rpm in high gear, and this should be factored into converter selection.

4. Before buying a new converter, consider all variables such as tire size, gear ratio, expected quarter-mile speed, maximum engine RPM (both physical and where the power begins to drop sharply), engine vacuum at idle, and engine torque at low RPM. All reputable suppliers will ask about these characteristics—and more—prior to selling a converter.

The correct converter selection will provide some minor creep in Drive at your normal idle speed and will allow normal acceleration in traffic without excessive slippage and high RPM. It will provide a constant speed on the road without noticeable engine RPM changes when climbing and descending hills.

When power is needed and the throttle is opened quickly, the correct converter will allow the engine to immediately move to a higher RPM range. At the drag strip, it may improve the ET (elapsed time), but still provides good MPH numbers. If your converter does not provide these characteristics, consider a custom-made unit, because it is possible to have it all.

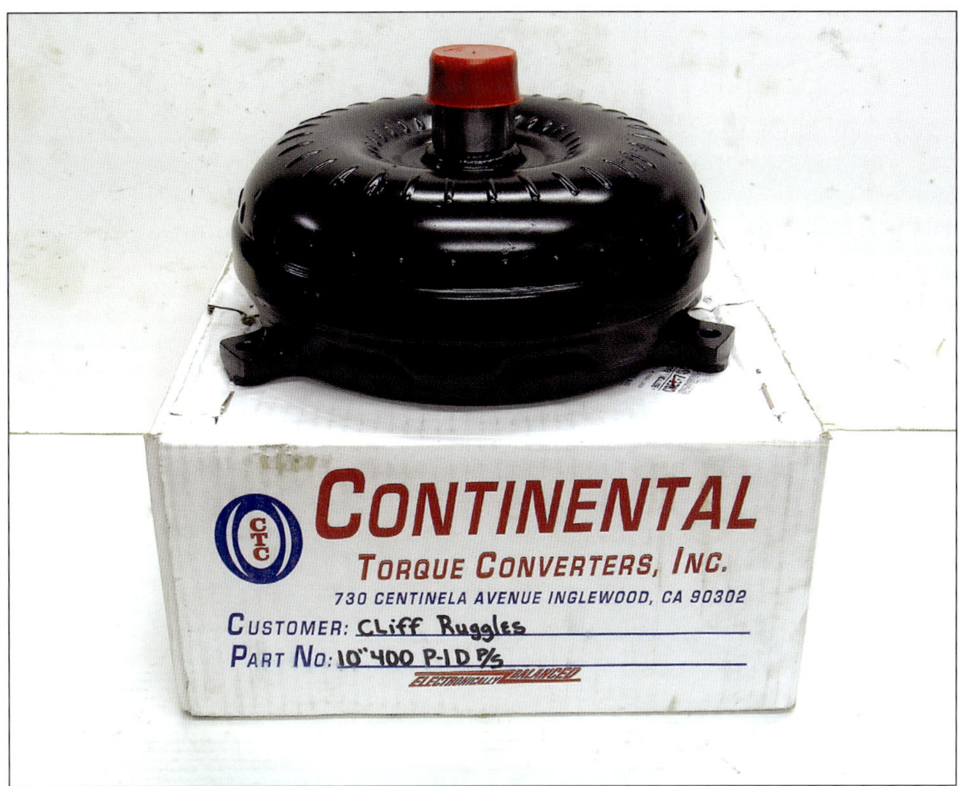

Several companies offer high-performance aftermarket torque converters. Continental Torque Converters in Inglewood, California, provided this 10-in custom unit. They are a company dedicated to providing the very best torque converters in the industry. Each unit is custom built for the application.

5. The torque-converter clutch can be used to cease all torque multiplication for drag racing, road racing, etc. Many racers will use the TCC as early as second gear to provide a direct coupling between the engine and rear axle once the vehicle has launched. This allows for a relatively loose converter to be used for maximum starting-line performance, and still see the benefits of full power transfer during the run, and lowest possible RPM at trap speeds. The problem with this is that the TCC is simply not strong enough in most stock or mildly modified converters to hold up to the power applied to it during the run. The aftermarket has stepped up with heavy-duty torque converters, with multiple-disk clutches and billet housings. For serious drag-strip use where the user intends on applying the TCC during the run, these stronger converters should be considered.

The multiple-disk clutch assemblies increase the amount of friction material to greatly increase holding power when the TCC is applied. The pump cover and pump assembly are made of much stronger materials, so they hold their shape better when the TCC is applied. These converters are available from most companies for applications where the user plans on using the TCC when the engine is making full power, and they want all of the power produced to go directly to the transmission. These converters are very expensive; some cost as much as or more than a complete high-performance overdrive transmission.

Transmission Removal and Installation

Removing and installing a transmission can be a difficult experience. Due to the weight of the unit, some sort of lifting apparatus is needed to lift it into place. The best scenario is to have the vehicle on a lift, and have access to a transmission jack. Since many of you don't have vehicle lifts and transmission jacks available, you may have to resort to other means.

Access to a vehicle hoist and shop-type transmission jack is far and away the best way to remove and install a transmission. Transmissions are heavy, and many vehicles will have a lot of other items under the chassis to remove in order to facilitate transmission removal and installation. It's always easier to stand under the vehicle than to lie on your back and work off of the floor.

Tips for Removing Transmissions

Safety is of the utmost concern when removing a transmission from a vehicle. To facilitate getting the transmission down and out of the vehicle, the vehicle needs to be raised off the ground and supported on floor jacks. Make sure the jacks are under the vehicle's frame and positioned out of the way so that a floor jack or transmission jack can be rolled under the vehicle without hitting them. The vehicle can also be placed on heavy-duty ramps, but it is still advisable to use a good set

Floor jacks should be placed under the frame of the vehicle once it has been raised into position. They should be positioned at equal height and parallel with each other to equally support the weight of the vehicle. Make sure to position the jack stands so they do not interfere with getting the transmission out from under the vehicle, or with the legs of an engine hoist, if one is used to support the engine during the procedure.

The inspection cover is used to keep dirt and debris away from the flywheel and torque converter. It must be removed to access the three torque-converter bolts that attach the torque converter to the flywheel. The engine's crankshaft will need to be turned to access the bolts. You may also need a large screwdriver to wedge between the flywheel teeth so that it doesn't turn while loosening the bolts.

of floor jacks under the frame for safety reasons.

Before attempting to remove the transmission-to-engine bolts, the torque converter must be unbolted from the flywheel. The inspection cover is removed first. This should provide access to the bolts; the engine will have to be turned to access them. A screwdriver can be used between the flywheel teeth and the edge of the transmission case (to keep it from turning) to break the bolts loose.

You will also need to remove the vehicle's driveshaft. The transmission fluid should be drained prior to removing the driveshaft, unless a spare yoke is available to slip into the transmission to prevent fluid leakage.

A spare transmission yoke can be inserted into the tail housing when the driveshaft is removed. This will keep transmission fluid from spilling out while it is being removed from the vehicle.

The transmission shift linkage must be disconnected. Some vehicles will use a cable that attaches to the transmission pan bolts. Many trucks and heavy-duty vehicles will use linkage coming across from the frame.

The speedometer cable can be removed with a pair of channel locks. It unscrews from the speedometer-gear housing. Later computerized vehicles may have wiring to disconnect instead, as they only used the reluctor on the tailshaft for a reference signal to provide the vehicle's speed at the speedometer. For 4WD applications, the speedometer cable or wiring is attached to the transfer case instead.

The rear transmission mount is bolted to the transmission crossmember. Some mounts use two bolts, others one bolt. The crossmember must be removed from most vehicles in order to remove the transmission. Once the transmission rear mount bolts have been removed, raise the transmission high enough to remove the crossmember. Some crossmembers are two or three pieces, and can be taken apart. Some have to be twisted and lowered from the frame rails after removing the attaching bolts.

Cooling lines can be difficult to access. On some vehicles, you may have to lower the transmission slightly to gain access to the cooling lines. Several different types of fittings were used; the most common is a 5⁄16-in inverted flare, requiring a ½-in tubing wrench to loosen them.

"H" and "X" pipes are popular in high-performance vehicles. Many times they will cross right under the transmission, and will have to be removed before lowering the transmission from the vehicle.

Remove any shift linkage attached to the transmission, and the speedometer cable or wiring. Disconnect the TCC wiring or wiring harness from 4L60E models.

The transmission cooling lines must be removed from the case. On some vehicles they may be difficult to access. They may also be difficult to loosen due to rust and corrosion from road salt. Worst-case scenario, the lines can be cut and replaced or the transmission lowered slightly to gain better access to the lines.

A bottle jack and wooden block can be used to support the engine under the oil pan. It is important to keep the engine from tilting back while the transmission is being removed. Some General Motors vehicles have so little clearance at the rear of the engine that the distributor cap will be crushed against the firewall if the engine is allowed to tilt during the procedure.

Move the transmission lift into place and strap the transmission to the lift if one is available. Remove the rear mounting bolts and raise the transmission to facilitate removal of the rear frame mount.

Some vehicles may also have exhaust systems that will need to be removed prior to removing the transmission.

The extreme heat that most exhaust systems see will usually have most of the fasteners heavily rusted. Plan on soaking most of the bracket, flange, and clamp bolts with penetrating oil before attempting to loosen them.

It is recommended to support the engine prior to removing the transmission bell-housing bolts. The exhaust system may support the engine in some applications, but a small bottle jack or engine lift is recommended to make sure the engine doesn't fall back far enough to break the distributor cap against the firewall. Some GM vehicles have very little clearance.

Remove the bell-housing bolts. The top bolts can be extremely difficult to access on some models. Some vehicles, such as late model Blazers and Suburbans, may also have studded bolts with nuts that hold various

A long 3/8-in extension and swivel 9/16-in socket can be very effective in getting to and removing the upper bell-housing bolts. The other alternative is laying over the engine and removing them a quarter-turn at a time with an open- or box-end wrench. If the swivel socket is flopping around too much, it can be wrapped with a piece of electrical tape. This will make it easier to guide onto the bolts from under the vehicle, and it will still swivel when removing them.

A plate can be made to turn a standard shop floor jack into a transmission jack. I have used this plate to remove scores of transmissions and transfer cases over the years. It may not reach high enough for all vehicles, but gets them close enough so I can wrestle them in the rest of the way.

If the transmission was not drained prior to removing it from the vehicle, place it in a holding fixture mounted to the workbench, and drain into a bucket or pan. Leave it in this position for at least 20 minutes. The torque converter can be removed and placed over a 5-gallon bucket to drain.

A new torque converter should be included for all rebuilt transmissions. Slowly add 1 or 2 quarts of fluid to the converter, and lubricate the seal surface with clean ATF or TransGel. Slide the converter into the transmission, while turning it at the same time. It will engage the input shaft, stator shaft, and then "clunk" into the oil pump. When correctly installed, there should be about ¼ in clearance between the back of the torque converter and the oil pump.

Adding Fluid

At least 1 quart of ATF should be added to the torque converter before it is installed into the transmission, and make sure to put some TransGel or petroleum jelly on the hub to lubricate the front seal. The converter will fill automatically when the engine is first started. Converters can hold quite a bit of fluid, and the installer must continue to add fluid to the transmission until the converter is full, and the fluid level in the pan is up to the lower level on the dipstick. The installer should add 4 quarts of ATF to the transmission at initial engine startup, and then continue to add fluid until the converter and transmission are full. Leave the fluid level on the dipstick to the lowest part of the range. Once this is accomplished, place the transmission shift selector into Drive, then into Reverse, and then back into Park. The vehicle should be raised with the rear wheels off the ground, and the parking brake locked. The fluid level should be checked again. It is best to leave the level at the lower part of the "add" mark on the dipstick, as the fluid level will increase when it gets hot. Check the fluid level again after the engine and transmission are completely warmed up, and add fluid as necessary.

The transmission dipstick shows the range of acceptable fluid level. When the transmission is first installed, add 4 quarts of ATF, then start the engine. Continue to add ATF, checking the level after each quart, until it comes onto the lower range on the dipstick. The transmission should* not *be placed in gear until you have established an acceptable fluid level in the pan with the engine running. Depending on the size of the torque converter used, this may take nearly a dozen quarts of fluid. Once the level is at the lower end of the range on the dipstick, place the transmission in gear, and then back to Park, and check the level again. Do not attempt to move the vehicle until the fluid level is in the safe range. It is best to leave the level a pint low, until the vehicle has been driven and the fluid fully warmed up. It usually expands enough to bring the level to the full mark.

other items in place behind the bell housing, such as the main wiring harness.

With the transmission securely supported on the jack, and all the transmission-to-engine bolts removed, pull the transmission back far enough so it can be lowered to the ground. It may be stuck pretty hard on the engine's dowel pins, and the converter hub may also be stuck in the rear of the engine's crankshaft. A long pry bar may be needed to help break things loose.

Make sure that the transmission doesn't tilt forward while being lowered to the ground, and that the filler tube remains seated in the unit. The torque converter can fall out if the unit tilts forward, and fluid will drain if the filler tube doesn't stay seated in the transmission.

Once on the ground, the torque converter can be removed to reduce weight and make the transmission easier to handle. Some fluid will be lost; remove the torque converter quickly and cover the opening to prevent any dirt from getting into the unit.

The transmission can now be bolted to your holding fixture and placed on the workbench. If not drained previously, turn the unit so the tail housing is pointing toward the ground, remove the slip yoke, and drain into a large pan or bucket. Leave the unit in this position for at least 20 minutes prior to taking it apart.

Tips for Installing Transmissions

Prior to installing the transmission into place, you need to make sure that the torque converter is fully engaged into the transmission stator, input shaft, and oil pump. With the transmission sitting on the pan, carefully install the torque converter. Spin the torque converter while pushing it

A small strap can be used to secure the transmission to your jack while positioning it under the vehicle. This will keep it from sliding off the jack while moving it into position, and can be left in place until you are ready to move the transmission into final position.

back towards the transmission. This will help to align the input shaft and stator splines. The transmission oil pump must also engage with the two notches in the converter hub. The torque converter will finally "clunk" into place when the two notches on the hub engage the transmission's oil pump. The converter may be difficult to get in the transmission when a new bushing is installed in the pump. This is normal, as the clearance between the parts is minimal.

For most installations, the transmission filler tube and dipstick will also need to be in the transmission. Some can be very difficult if not impossible to install once the transmission is bolted to the engine, as there may be little if any room between the transmission bell housing and the vehicle firewall. Don't find this out after the transmission has been bolted in place.

The rear transmission mount should also be bolted into place, and the bolts torqued to specifications with a drop of blue Loctite on them.

The transmission is now ready to raise into position. Make sure that the transmission is securely fastened to the transmission jack, and tilted back slightly while being raised into position. Line up the boltholes and the dowel-pin holes, and carefully slide the transmission in place.

Transmission Alignment

A couple of ⅜ x 16 bolts can be modified to help guide the transmission into place. Place the bolts in a vise, and use soft jaws or protect the threads with a piece of cardboard or leather. Cut the heads off the bolts. With a hacksaw, cut a slot in the top of each bolt. Grind the head off each stud with a slight taper. These guide studs can be inserted into the engine to help guide the transmission into position. A flat-tip screwdriver can be used to remove them once a couple of bolts have been installed to hold the transmission to the bell housing.

A couple of ⅜-in bolts can be used as guide pins to help align the transmission to the engine. Cut the heads off of them with a hacksaw, and then grind them to a dull point with a bench grinder. Secure them in a vise, and cut a slot in the ends with a hacksaw. This will allow you to use a flat-tip screwdriver to remove them after sliding the transmission into place.

Transmission Model Gear Ratios—Critical Measurements

GM Transmissions	1st	2nd	3rd	4th	OVERALL LENGTH	BELLHOUSING-TO-MOUNT
TH700-R4/4L60	3.06	1.62	1.00	0.70	23⅜*	22⅜*
TH200-4R	2.74	1.57	1.00	0.67	27¾	26⅞
4L60E	3.06	1.62	1.00	0.70	30¾	22⅜
4L80E	2.48	1.48	1.00	0.75	31½	30⅜
TH350	2.52	1.52	1.00	N/A	27⅝**	20⅜
TH400	2.48	1.48	1.00	N/A	28¼***	26¾

The chart above provides specifics for the most popular General Motors rear-wheel-drive transmissions. It can be used to compare gear ratios for rear-end ratio selection. The transmission's overall length and rear-mount position also show where driveshaft lengths will require a longer or shorter driveshaft. Also note that the rear transmission-mount location is different, and will also require relocation, or at least some modification.

Aftermarket Torque Converters

Aftermarket torque converters may use a different mounting-bolt arrangement from stock units. Most stock converters will have threads for the attaching bolts. Many aftermarket high-performance converters will use a much stronger mount, which may require larger bolts and nuts. Make sure the flywheel holes have been enlarged accordingly if using an aftermarket converter that requires larger bolts. Don't find this out after the transmission has been bolted in place.

Some aftermarket torque converters may not use the standard bolt locations. Smaller torque converters often use a smaller bolt circle on the flywheel. They may also require bolts and nuts, instead of the factory-style attaching bolts. If larger bolts are required, make sure to drill the flywheel to accommodate them before bolting the transmission in place.

Once the transmission has been guided into place over the engine dowel pins, install one bolt on each side. Before tightening either bolt, make sure that the transmission is flush with the engine, and that the torque converter will spin freely. If the torque converter will not turn, it may not be correctly engaged in the oil pump. If the bolts to the engine are tightened at this point, the oil pump will be severely damaged.

Install and tighten all the transmission-to-engine bolts. Raise the transmission to facilitate installing the crossmember and rear mount bolts. Turn the engine and install the flywheel-to-converter bolts. It is best to install all the bolts and leave them about a half-turn loose, then tighten them correctly the next time around. If one bolt is tightened and the others not started, there may be alignment problems and the other bolts may not start.

Hook up the cooling lines, shift linkage, and speedometer cable or wiring. Connect the wiring harness to the transmission. Make sure the rear wheels are off the ground, the parking brake is locked, and the transmission shifter is in Park. The engine can now be started, and the transmission topped off with fluid. Check for leaks while the engine is warming up and continue to add fluid until the transmission is full.

If no leaks are found, and the fluid level is full, place the transmission in Drive while holding the brakes. Place the selector into Reverse, then back into Park, and re-check the fluid level. Add fluid as needed, and repeat this procedure a couple of times. The operator should feel the transmission engage and place some load on the engine.

CHAPTER 7

Swapper's Guide

By Ro McGonegal

At first, the idea of adding an overdrive feature was novel to hot rodders and enthusiasts, but it is now another piece of must-have equipment for the complete car. Original equipment manufacturers were way ahead of hot rodders in this instance, having put overdrive in production vehicles for more than 25 years. Detroit actually learned something from the fuel-rationing debacles in 1973 and 1979. Hence, the market was ready for the hop-up guys before there even was a market, corporate average fuel economy (CAFE) notwithstanding. Much later, the advent and press coverage of popular over-the-road gatherings, such as the Hot Rod Power Tour, stressed the importance of this auxiliary gearing and in today's gas-crunch climate overdriven top gears have become mandatory equipment.

Step-by-Step Swap: TH350 to TH700-R4

Although possible to do in your driveway, it is much easier if the car is on a lift. If you must do this operation on the ground, support the vehicle with jack stands at all four corners. These transmissions are very heavy, hold many quarts of fluid, and wiggle room is scant, so regardless of your method, you must use a proper transmission jack to support the case and to move it back and forth. Before you begin, disconnect the battery, the throttle valve (TV) cable from the carburetor or EFI and the hold-down bracket, remove the distributor cap, and place the shift lever in Neutral. Raise the car. Note: Powerglide, TH350 and TH400 transmissions use vacuum control to perform the upshift. The 700-R4, 200-4R, etc., do this via the cable-operated TV. (Information for and swap performed by Monster Transmission & Performance: www.eatmyshift.com.)

You can delete some of the transmission mass (approximately 25 pounds) immediately by dropping the pan and draining the fluid. Have the correct plastic plug or a spare yoke to cap the output shaft to keep the fluid from draining out once the driveshaft has been extracted. Have a bucket ready. Now you are ready to begin.

Disconnect the shift linkage from the transmission and move it aside or tie it out of the way. If the shifter is an aftermarket item, the procedure is still the same.

Using a 7/16 wrench, remove the U-bolts holding the driveshaft universal joint to the differential yoke. Be careful to retain the bearing cups and keep the roller bearings intact.

Pull the driveshaft back and out of the tailshaft. Have that spare yoke or the proper size plastic cap ready to put over (or in) the tailshaft to keep the fluid from draining out.

Three bolts hold the torque converter to the flywheel (flexplate). Transmissions manufactured in 1975 and earlier used 9/16 bolt head and 3/8 x 16 threads. Later models used metric fasteners with a 15mm bolt head x 10mm x 1.5 thread. Using a pry bar, rotate the flywheel to access the bolts.

The 3/8-inch bolts that secure this ('68 Camaro) transmission crossmember are accessed by holes in the sub-frame. Remove them now.

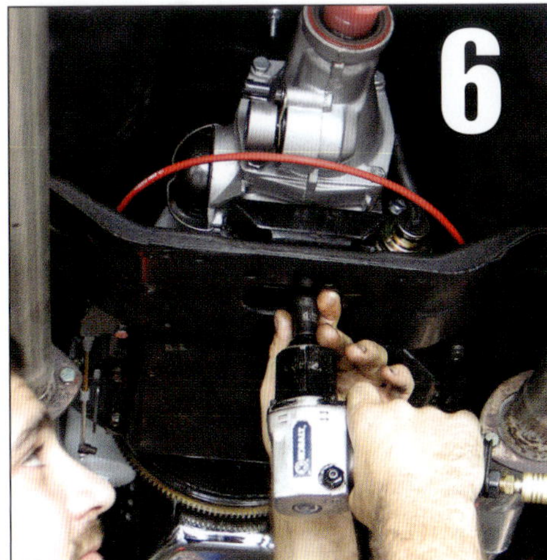

Early cars, like this one, used a two-bolt (3/8 x 16 thread x 1.25-in) transmission mounting pad. Later ones (approximately 1982-up) used a single bolt (10mm x 1.5 x 1.25-in) for the pad-to-crossmember attachment. If the mount shows any sign of wear, replace it with a new OE assembly or stronger one from the aftermarket.

Position the four locating tabs on the transmission jack beneath the pan so that the weight of the case is distributed evenly. Raise the jack slightly to take the weight off the crossmember.

Remove the crossmember. This may require a strong arm and a hammer.

Now unhook the speedometer cable, vacuum lines, and the linkage and move them out of the way. Put another jack under the engine oil pan to keep rearward tilt at a minimum once the transmission support has been removed. Remove the shift arm from the TH350 transmission. Early ones (1981-earlier) are secured with a ⅜-inch nut.

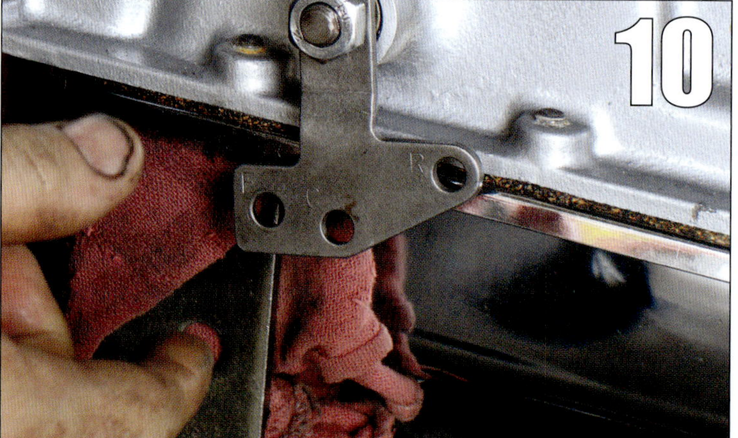

Shift arm attachment on later production units used a metric 10mm X 1.5 thread nut.

Remove the dipstick.

Plug the hole with the proper plastic stopper (PN CP-7A). An old spark plug and a rag will accomplish the same thing.

Sometimes it's easier to get at the top three of the six ⅜ x 2-in bellhousing bolts from above before the car goes on the hoist. If not, you'll need a ½-in ratchet, a long extension, a swivel socket, and foul oathes.

There are two coolant line fittings and one detent/TV cable port. There are also four threaded holes on the right side of the transmission case. Pivot the loosened transmission to the side to access them. Have the proper plugs on hand to staunch fluid leak. The transmission is now ready to be removed.

Slide the transmission/jack rearward and lower it to working height (bench). Pull the torque converter loose and slide it out. Drain the fluid from the converter as well as the transmission (if not already done).

Plug the vacuum hole in the carburetor or the port in the EFI with a cap.

Install the TV cable. (Black unit directly below the throttle cable). Note: Powerglide, TH350 and TH400 transmissions use a vacuum controller to up-shift the gears.

Push the end of the TV cable through the hole in the mounting bracket.

To prevent the end of the cable from ever becoming dislodged, secure the end in the bracket with a tie-wrap to keep the tabs permanently open.

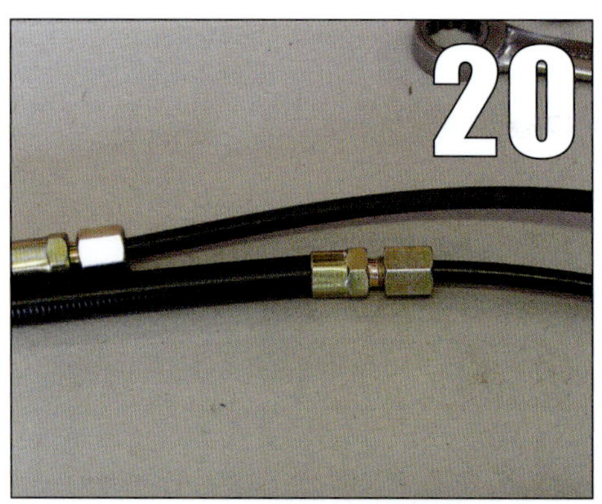

The 700-R4 TV cable (bottom) has a larger diameter than that of the TH350. The Monster Transmission unit shown here is fully adjustable for length.

The rubber grommet at the end of the cable housing (not the cable itself) must first be pressed in the transmission case prior to installation of the TV cable.

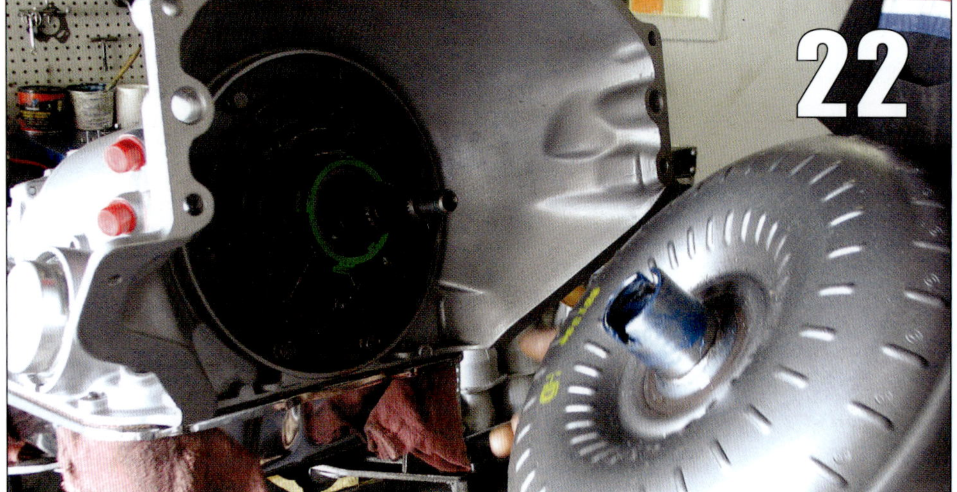

Monster used a new torque converter that they pre-lubed with one quart of transmission fluid before installation. The business end of the converter has already been lubed (blue grease). Thread type changes from standard coarse to metric fine on the new converter (10mm x 14.295mm x 1.5mm).

The 700-R4 input shaft has three steps, the largest of which is to accommodate the converter lock-up feature.

Gently push the converter on the shaft and spin it clockwise so that the pump stator aligns with the splines on the converter. Then you'll feel a second clunk as the hub aligns with the gear. If you don't here or feel the clunk, begin the procedure again until you do. (See Sidebar: "Hub of the Universe.")

You're ready to put the transmission back on the engine. Invariably, the unit will have to be wiggled into place because it won't couple up by going straight in. As precaution, attach a hold-down strap to the transmission and jack. Flexplates for TH350 and 700-R4 are identical.

Thread type changes from standard coarse to metric fine on the new converter (10mm x 14.30 x 1.5mm). Some converters also require nut and bolt.

Re-attach all the lines, shifter cable, and speedometer cable (the one for TH350 and 700-R4 are identical) before you bolt the transmission to the engine. Since line-pressure control is built into the 700-R4 transmission, there's no need for a ground or a hot lead.

The 700-R4 stock oil pan is 2 ⅜-in longer than that of the TH350. Be prepared to trim the crossmember to accommodate.

Use a grease pencil to mark and egg-out the existing transmission mount holes as shown and loosely apply the member to the sub-frame.

Depending on the vehicle, a www.shiftworks.com conversion unit allows you to run either a column shift or a floor shift. Monster prefers the B&M MegaShifter (PN 80690) because it is simple and trouble-free.

You might also have to modify the crossmember to fit the fluid pan. Make similar traces on the cross-member and remove the offending portion with cut-off wheels. Dress with a file. Drill a second set of attachment holes 2 ⅜ in to the rear on the sub-frame.

The trimmed and dressed crossmember fits the Monster fluid pan like it was made for it.

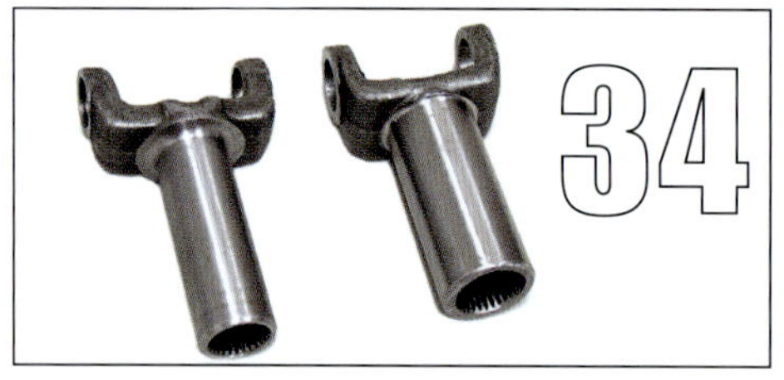

All GM automatics, save for the TH400, use the same 27-spline slip-joint. Since the 700-R4 is longer than that of the TH350 yoke, the driveshaft may need to be shortened to accommodate.

Reinstall the transmission filler tube, add one container of Lube Guard, and then fill the transmission with fluid.

Adjustment of the TV cable is critical. Failure to do so will burn out the clutches in a matter of minutes. Make sure the action of the cable-pull is level. The rear section of the TV is where you fine tune the adjustment for the proper shift points and the lock tab in the center is where you adjust it in or out.

Monster 700-R4 is in and ready to rock, but first...

...after the basic adjustment, you'll need to road test it. Under part-throttle, the 1-2 shift should occur between 16 to 20 mph. If the transmission shifts too early, remove some of the slack from the cable. If it shifts late, put a little more slack in the line.

This heavily customized '64 GTO rides on a tube frame, Corvette C5 suspension, and is powered by a 5.7L Corvette engine hooked to a 4L60E transmission.

Hub of the Universe

The hub of the torque converter is notched so that the converter can be pulled back to align with the flywheel. The pump gear fits into these notches. Misalignment causes immediate fracture and failure of the gear, so be careful.

Torque Converters and Camshaft Events

Before choosing a torque converter, you must evaluate your engine and car combination along with your performance expectations. For an engines with relatively mild camshaft events, look for a converter that provides a bit more stall speed (RPM) to coincide with the power band produced by the new cam. The keys are camshaft lift and duration. You must also know how much horsepower and torque your engine makes and the power band at which these occur. Dynamometer testing (engine or chassis) will tell you this. If your engine is equipped with a long-duration cam, low-speed torque will suffer, and more stall speed will be necessary to increase the engine's performance. Use the following as rule-of-thumb to help in choosing the correct converter stall speed for your car.

GROSS LIFT	DURATION	SBC (rpm)	BBC (rpm)
0.400-0.440	200-240	1,650	1,300-1,600
0.450-0.470	230-260	1,800-2,000	1,600-1,900
0.480-0.510	260-290	2,300-2,500	1,800-2,300
0.510-0.540	260-290	2,400-2,800	2,200-2,500
0.520-0.580	290-340	2,800-3,200	2,500-2,800
0.570-0.600	290-380	3,300-3,500	2,800-3,300

GM used two types of torque converter-to flexplate fasteners. Black bolt (left) is metric (10-mm x 14.3 x 1.5-in) with corresponding nut. Gold bolt (right) is standard GM (3/8 x 1/2 x 16 coarse).

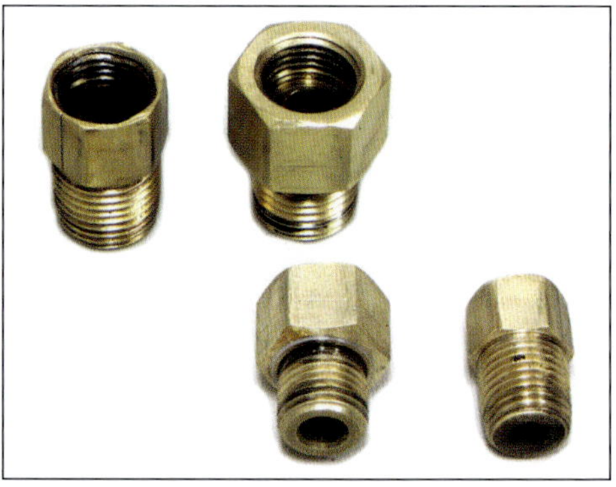

Thread size for all cooling lines in all GM transmissions are identical (5/16 x 1/4 pipe thread). During 1973–'74 model year, GM enlarged the head of the fitting to discourage corners from being rounded off and rendering them useless. Large head version (left) was used on TH350, TH400, 700-R4, 4L60 through '96. Thereafter, the fittings were converted to a snap-in type connector.

Swap Parts Guide

Though the notion seems simple enough—take one transmission out and replace it with another of a similar nature, albeit electronically controlled—it is never what it appears to be. Will the bellhousing attachment holes correspond with the ones on the back of the block? Will the driveshaft bolt back in? Will the crossmember accommodate the swap? What about the cooling lines? Is the hardware compatible? Where do you begin the reassembly? Before you begin, seriously consider using new fasteners for the project that are available from any GM dealer or from an aftermarket source.

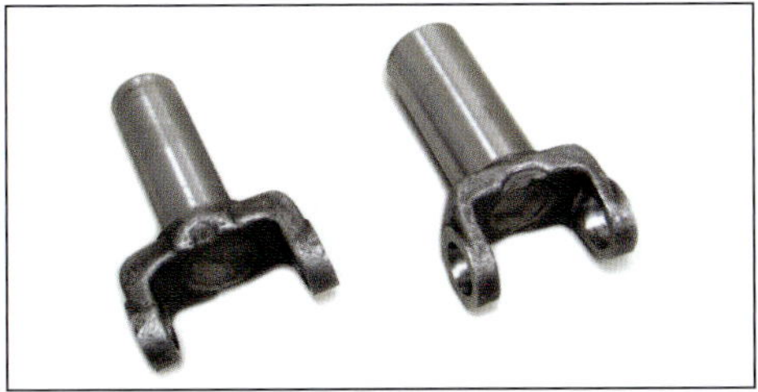

Driveshaft yoke for a 700-R4, 200-4R, 4L60, 4L60E, etc. (on the left) has 27-splines and is obviously narrower than the 4L80E yoke.

The TH400/4L80E yoke has 32-splines and has considerable heft and girth compared to the lesser yoke.

The bellhousing is connected to the back of the block via six (sometimes five, depending on transmission type) with 3/8 x 16 coarse, x 1-1/2 standard-thread bolts.

Small silver bolts secure the shift detent cable and speedometer bracket on the transmission tail shaft.

Standard GM replacement shows three mounting holes. Depending on the year of the vehicle, two outer threaded holes secure the transmission tailshaft to the crossmember. Later model tail shafts use only the center hole.

If you're going to get rough with the car, then perhaps a sturdier polyurethane mount (in this case Energy Suspension) would be in order. Tailshaft bolt pattern and crossmember attachment is identical to OE piece.

The vital link: top driveshaft is an aluminum unit used for Powerglide, TH350, 700-R4 and 200-4R with a 27-spline yoke. The second unit, also with a 27-spline yoke, is for 4L60E and 4L65E. Bottom prop shaft is TH400 or 4L80E type with 32-spline output shaft. In many cases, the transmission you're swapping in for a TH350 or TH400 will have a longer tailshaft than the OE unit thus requiring the services of a competent driveshaft shop to shorten (and rebalance) it the appropriate (3 inches or less) amount.

Cruise RPM Charts

Though the possibilities presented by ring-and-pinion ratios, transmission overdrive ratio, tire height, etc., are nearly infinite, we've included some of the most used and most popular sizes and gearing. One is for passenger cars; the other is for light-duty trucks.

Popular GM Transmissions (OD Ratios)

Transmission	OD Ratio
TH350	1:1
TH400	1:1
200-4R	0.67
700-R4	0.70
4L60E	0.70
4L80E	0.70

Trucks

Tire	Height	Final Drive	RPM*
225/70/15	27.4	3.08:1	1,851
225/70/16	28.4	3.31:1	1,919
275/60/17	30.0	3.42:1	1,877
285/60/18	31.5	3.73:1	1,950
285/50/18	29.3	4.10:1	2,304
275/45/20	29.8	4.10:1	2,265

**All running at 70 mph with a 0.70:1 OD*

Cars

Tire	Height	Final Drive	RPM/0.67:1 OD	RPM/0.70:1 OD
225/50/16	25.0	2.73:1	1,721	1,798
245/40/16	24.7	3.08:1	1,965	2,053
255/40/16	25.0	3:31:1	2,086	2,180
275/40/17	25.7	3.42:1	2,090	2,191
275/40/18	26.7	3.73:1	2.201	2,300
295/35/18	26.1	4.10:1	2,475	2,586

Bellhousing Bolt Pattern Identification

200-4R
The bellhousing pattern is B-O-P (Buick-Olds-Pontiac) but it also accommodates the small-bock Chevrolet "corporate" small-block. It is 27 11⁄16-in long and is 19 1⁄8-in wide at the block. Gear ratios: 2.78:1, 1.57:1, 1.00:1, 0.67:1. The 200-4R has an 11-bolt oil pan.

700-R4
GM incorporated the 700-R4 from 1982 to 1992. It has an overall length of 30 3⁄4 in. The bellhousing span is 18 1⁄4 in. Gear ratios: 3.06:1, 1.63:1, 1.00:1, 0.70:1. The 700-R4 has a 16-bolt oil pan. In 1993, its designation was changed to 4L60.

4L60/4L60E
In 1994, the 4L60E used a one-piece bellhousing and retained it through 1997 model year. It has the same dimensions and gear ratios as the 700-R4. GM introduced the Gen-III 5.7-liter small-block (LS) in the '97 Corvette. The 4L60E as used behind 4.8L, 5.3L, 5.7L, and 6.0L Gen-III engines.

TH400
There are two styles: B-O-P and Chevrolet. Depending on length of tail shaft, these big guys come in the following lengths: 28 3⁄8, 33 27⁄32 and 37 7⁄8 in). Gear ratios: 2.48:1, 1.48:1, 1.00:1. The TH400 has a 13-bolt oil pan.

TH350
Fits B-O-P and Chevrolet bolt-pattern. Various tail shafts extend length from (shortest) 27 11⁄16 to 33 27⁄32 in. Bellhousing span is 19 1⁄8 in. Gear ratios: 2.52:1, 1.52:1, 1.00:1. The TH350 has 13-bolt oil pan. (Note: Photo is Chevrolet only.)

4L60E, 4L65E
For the influx of brand new GM small-block engines, the 4L60E/4L65E (late '96 through '99) went to a 2-piece bellhousing. It has a 16-bolt oil pan and an 18 1⁄4-in span. Gear ratios: 3.06:1, 1.63:1, 1.00:1, 0.70:1

Links to Monster Transmission (case ID, bolt patterns, fluid pans patterns, etc.)
Transmission Case Dimensions (with printer friendly option):
http://racetransmissions.com/mainpages/tech_info/trans_dimensions/index.html
Transmission Gear Ratios: http://racetransmissions.com/mainpages/tech_info/trans_gear_ratios/index.html
Transmission Fluid Capacity: http://racetransmissions.com/mainpages/tech_info/trans_fluid/index.html
Identify Transmission Guide: http://racetransmissions.com/mainpages/tech_info/identify_your_trans/index.html

Electronic Transmission Controllers

As the market has become privy to many more variations of electronically controlled automatics, it was only natural for hot rodders to step in and enhance all the processes for increased efficiency, better performance and "feel," all without sacrificing an ounce of reliability. There are six such companies that provide similar services, all of them engineered with experience in high-tech industries (read aerospace as well as OE), the best equipment, the latest technology, and by the propulsion of years of hot-rod savvy.

Powertrain Control Solutions

Powertrain Control Solutions (PCS) offers a product to control electronic transmissions both in new and custom-built cars and light-duty trucks. The PCS universal controller is a fully programmable system via a PC Windows interface and users are able to program transmission settings based on ground speed, engine load, engine speed, and other parameters. This unit allows users to control every type of GM electronic automatic transmission.

The PCS mainstay is the D200, a unit capable of bringing together all the information on a vehicle from almost any input system for monitoring, data logging, and analysis. It is useful for stock as well as heavily modified vehicles as it sources information from Lambda meter, aftermarket ECU, transmission controller, fuel controller, MAP sensor, throttle position sensor, vehicle speed and more. These attributes are displayed by a large and easily viewable—even in direct sunlight—LCD touch-screen.

Powertrain Control Solutions, LLC
Ashland, VA 23005
804 752-6025
www.powertraincontrolsolutions.com

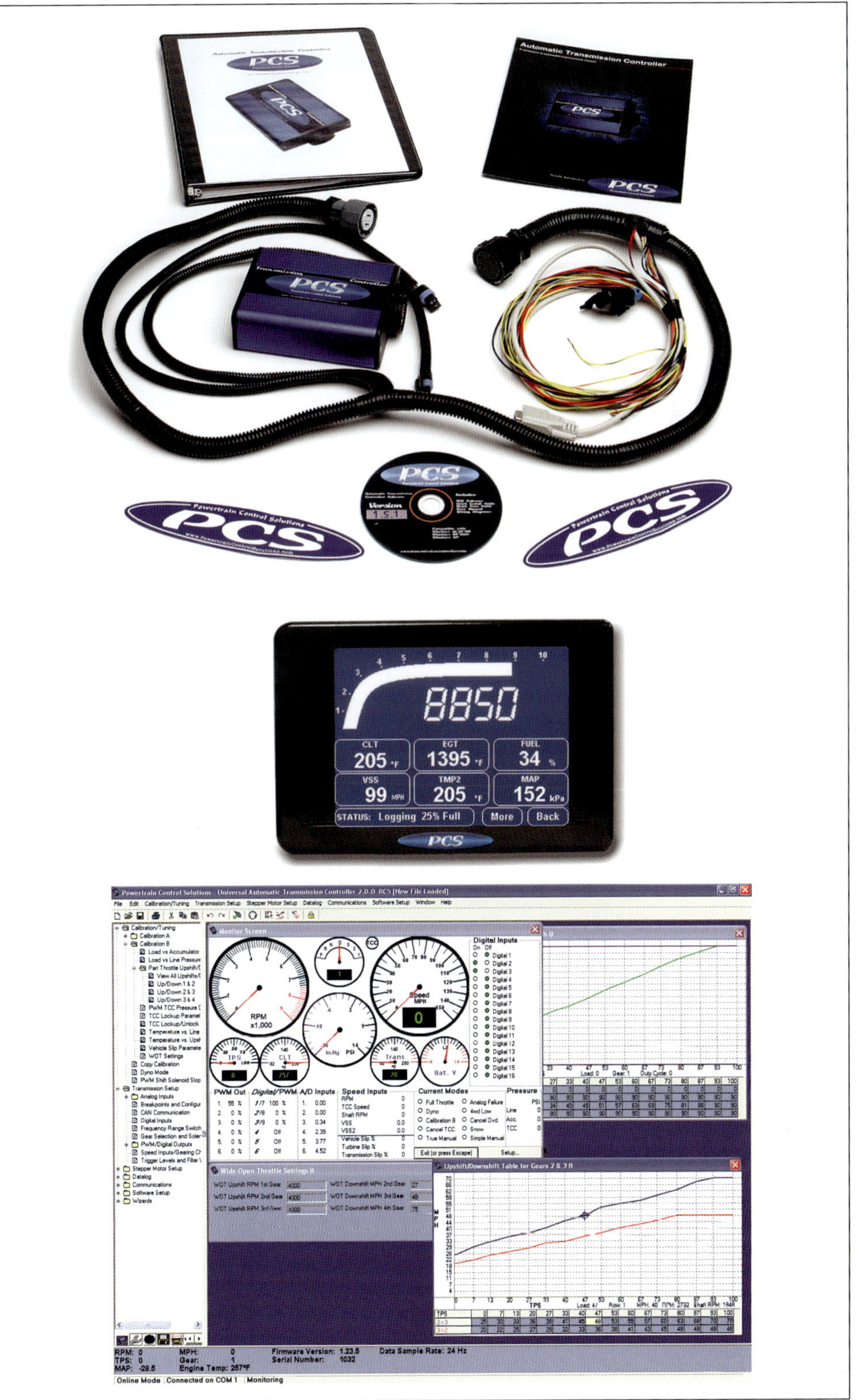

GM Performance Parts

The GMPP transmission controller (PN 12497316) for 4L60E, 4L65E, 4L80E, 4L85E) includes wiring harness, software, and laptop computer connector and allows complete programming of shifting, as well as part-throttle, wide open throttle, and shift firmness control. The unit is pre-programmed so all you have to do is enter the diameter of the rear tires. Wiring harness PN 124894 is included.

The GMPP transmission adapter kit (PN 19154766) is a tidy collection that lets you adapt any Gen-III or Gen-IV 4L60E or 4L80E transmission to a Gen-I or Gen-II engine. It comes complete with spacer ring (transmission-to-cylinder block adapter), shims, dowels, bolts, and flexplate. Be aware that it works only with one-piece rear main seal engines.

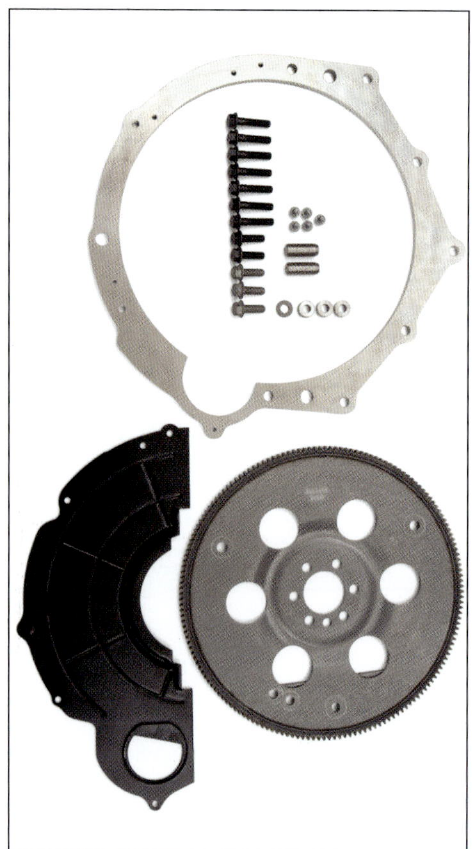

If you want to mate Gen-I style transmissions (TH350/400, 700R4, 4L60, 4L60E, or 4L85E) with a Gen-III or Gen-IV engine, you can do so with the crankshaft spacer (PN 12563532). Longer bolts (PN 12553332) are required.

GM Performance Parts
www.gmperformanceparts.com

Turbo Action

Turbo Action's controller is a complete Digital Smart Design EEProm Memory Computer from a company that's been producing drag-race oriented automatics for more than 30 years. The Turbo Action Cheetah E-shift controls RPM-activated devices such as air shifters, shift lights, electric shifters and electronic valve bodies, nitrous systems, throttle stops, burnout high RPM limiters, and many other applications. The controller features four outputs, handles five shifts, is time-based and includes a tachometer read-out. It includes race, burnout, transbrake and pit road return modes mode as well as hold/release relays. It automatically resets, contains virtual memory, is tamper-proof, and comes with a one-year warranty. It's also legal for NHRA and IHRA competition.

Turbo Action, Inc.
Jacksonville, FL 32218
904 741-4850
www.turboaction.com

TCI Transmission Control Unit

TCI's new Transmission Control Unit (TCU) for the 4L60E, 4L65E, 4L70E, 4L80E, and 4L85E includes Dual Tune Technology and paddle/button shifter capability. As the original TCU offered power and economy modes of operation, the Dual Tune unit allows you to create two completely different shift modes, including shift points and line pressure to increase shift firmness, all enhanced by an on-screen wizard that makes it easy to set up and navigate. The TCU is can be run as a standalone unit, even with a non-computer controlled engine, or in conjunction with OEM or aftermarket engine computers. Included is an array of tuning options including load, gear, RPM, and speed-based programming, all of which can be adjusted by simply connecting the unit to any Windows-based PC or laptop. (NOTE: If you have the 37000 controller you must use T-COM WP software, as the T-COM Version 2.0.1 will *not* work.

Its ability to communicate with the FAST XFI fuel injection system and other compatible CAN 2.0b devices means that the TCU uses a simpler, easier to install wiring harness than most other aftermarket transmission controllers. The unit includes friendly T-Com software, which allows simple plug-and-play transmission operation via several built-in programs, as well as custom tuning and programming, data logging, and fault diagnosis. A multitude

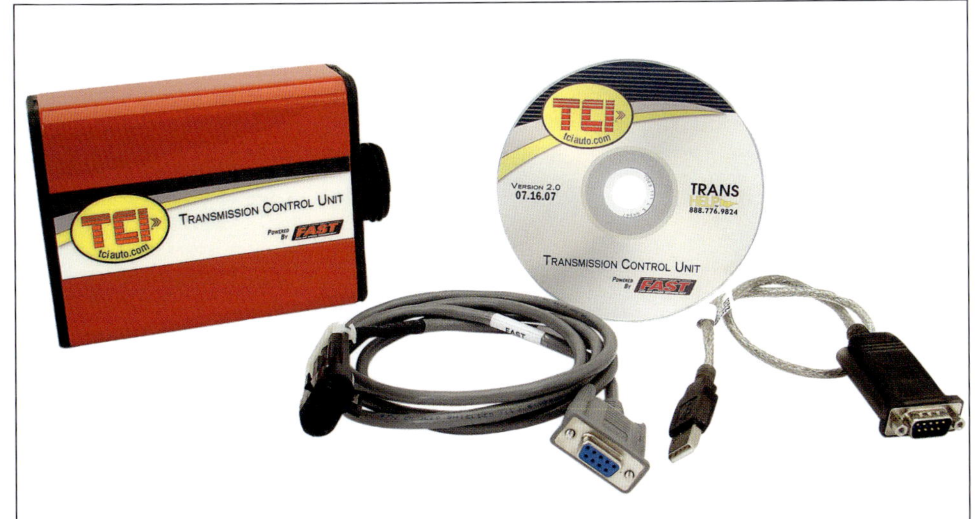

of digital inputs and outputs, analog inputs, and speed inputs and outputs allows the TCU to be custom tweaked to fit any requirement in a drag race application or manifold pressure-based shift firmness in a turbocharged application.

TCI wiring harnesses are pre-assembled and tested, making it easy to install even the most advanced computer-controlled transmission. The harnesses feature OEM-style connectors, high temperature oil resistant wiring and puncture-resistant outer sheathing. All connections are butt-connected, crimped, soldered, and are clearly labeled.

TCI
Ashland, MS 38603
888 776-9824
www.tciauto.com

HGM Electronics

COMPUSHIFT is a state-of-the-art transmission control system designed by HGM Automotive Electronics Inc. It is designed to operate automatic shifting and torque converter lock-up functions for a variety of transmissions, including the 4L60E transaxle in C5 and C6 Corvettes. At its heart is a digital signal processor that runs the COMPUSHIFT software. The cool thing is that it does not require a laptop, a PC or any other kind of computer to program the unit. The system is delivered with factory-set programming capable of dealing with all modes and includes all the necessary cable harnesses and a throttle position sensor. This system supports gasoline as well as diesel-fueled engines.

Optional equipment includes a liquid crystal or vacuum fluorescent display, a throttle position sensor re-fit kit, a cable-actuated Acculink throttle position sensor, Acculink bracket for a Lokar throttle cables (including a cruise control cable), and a crank speed sensor.

The system design incorporates a high-speed digital signal processor using COMPUSHIFT software that has pre-programmed shift and pressure tables, proprietary shift algorithms, built-in diagnostics (and optional display controller software). Simple adjustments and calibration can also be affected with a screwdriver and a pushbutton. A non-volatile memory stores calibration and programming information, and its printed circuit board can be upgraded in the field as well as at the factory.

The torque converter clutch lock and unlock are based on the position of the throttle, actual road speed, and gear selected. Users are able to adjust lock is based on road speed, unlock on the basis of throttle position, or lock based on gear the transmission is in. Operating modes include never, third, and high gear, and high gear only. A screwdriver is all that is needed to change the shift-speed adjustment and shift pressure potentiometer. A single TPS calibration switch is also part of the deal.

Electrical specs are 8 to 16 volts DC; a supply current of 600mA @ 14.4 volts and a maximum of 5A @ 14.4 volts (depending on transmission type); six solenoids are provided with automatic short-circuit protection. System is protected for internal shutdown for over-temperature and provides automatic protection against a failed solenoid(s).

HGM Electronics
Torrance, CA 90505
310 465-0220
www.hgmelectronics.com

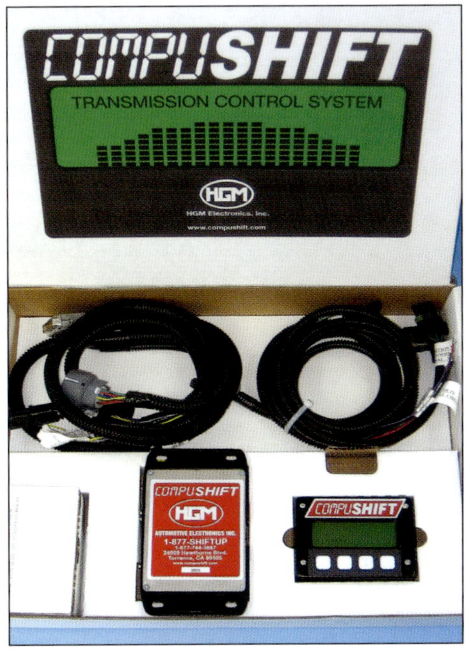

Essentially, the ATCB is a tuning tool that keeps the transmission from messing up the tuning process by hunting for gears on the upshift and downshift cycles. Look at the graph: the keyword here is smooth. It also allows the operator to make quick evaluations (e.g., reprogramming shift points, etc.) either on the street or at the dragstrip, thus eliminating the need to re-flash the CPU.

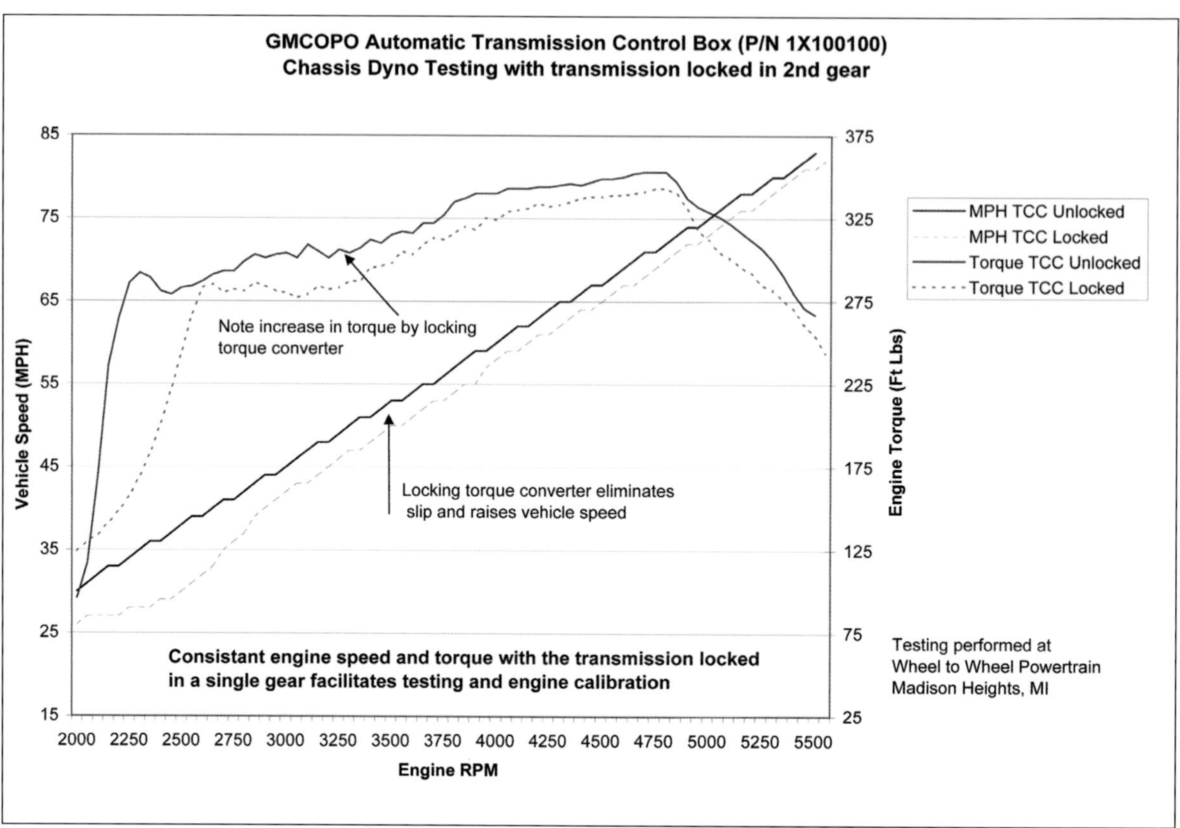

The first test was made "free range." Without the ATCB to monitor RPM and hold the transmission in second gear, you can see how very erratic the torque curve and engine speed plots become.

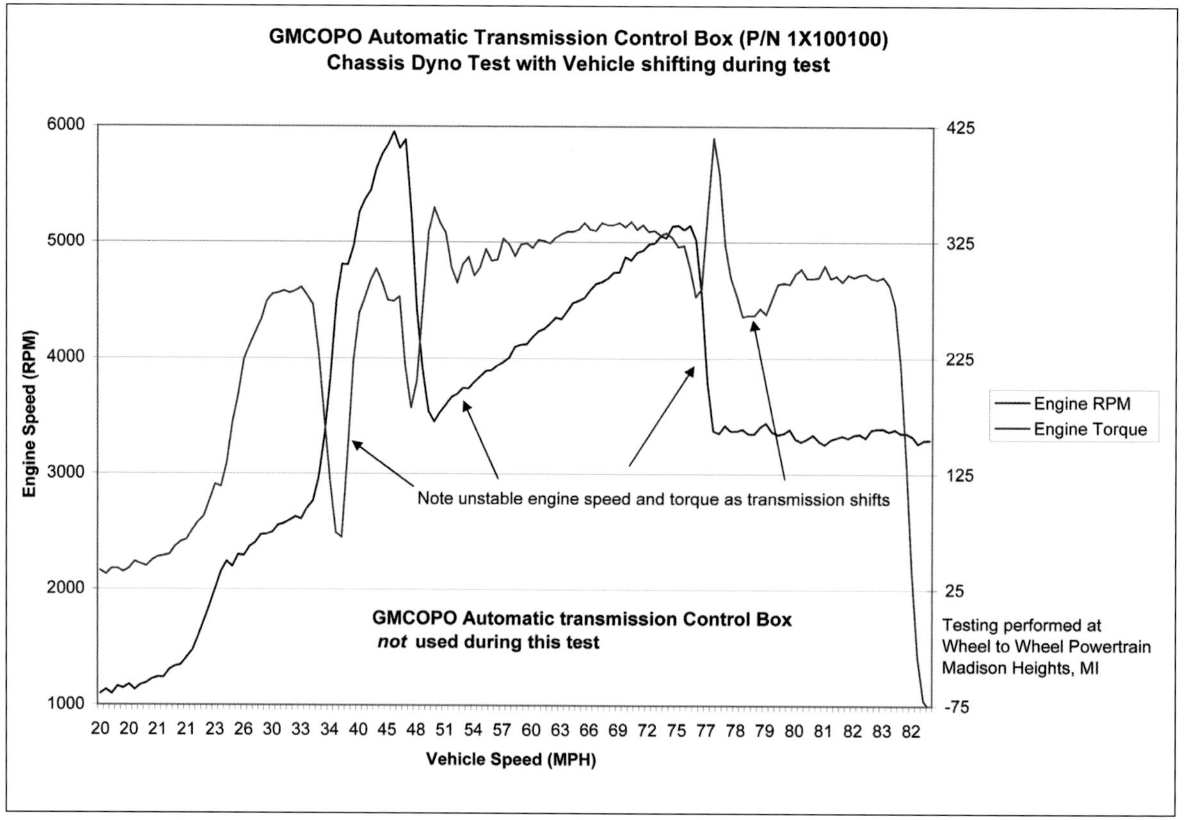

GMCOPO Controller (not affiliated with GM Corp.)

You know the frustration. That last bit of control and calibration eludes you like a greased pig. If you only had a pluck-your-magic-twanger box to give your stuff a sliver more information or confirmation that'll make it run smoother and more effectively than the next guy's.

Apply the GMCOPO Automatic Transmission Control Box (ATCB) to a 4L60E transmission and then lock it in second gear to prevent up or downshifting during the test. Locking the transmission in a single gear allows for a more consistent measurement of engine torque and at a lower engine speed.

The ATCB is a multi-tasking device able to apply the torque converter clutch, which facilitates calibration of ignition timing and A/F ratios over a broader range of engine speeds and throttle openings. It means that you can also determine torque output below the stall speed of the converter and quickly evaluate a variety of shift and converter lock-up points. Simply, the ATCB affords the ability to choose the gear as well as the moment the torque converter is applied for any GM electronic four-speed automatic, including front-wheel drive cars.

As a kit, the ATCB includes the control box (with torque converter control) and gear selector, a 6-foot power cord that plugs into the cigarette lighter, two 12-foot control harnesses: one for the 4T40E transaxle and 4L80/85E and the other for the 4T65E transaxle and 4L60/65/70E transmissions. A foam-padded carrying case holds it all. Adjunct to the electronically controlled transmissions, the ATCB can also be adapted to lock up the converter clutch of the TH125C, 200C, 2004R, 3T40, 350C, and 700R4/4L60 transmissions.

GMCOPO Factory Engineered Performance
248 275-5828
Auburn Hills, MI 48321
www.gmcopo.com

Transmission Swap Charts

All charts demonstrate engine RPM at varied road speed with the transmission in High gear. The Powerglide (2-speed), and TH350 and TH400 (3-speed) have 1:1 final drives. Overdrive automatics such as the 700-R4 (0.70:1) and 200-4R (0.67:1) cruise at the same speed as the non-OD equipped transmission but at markedly lower engine speed

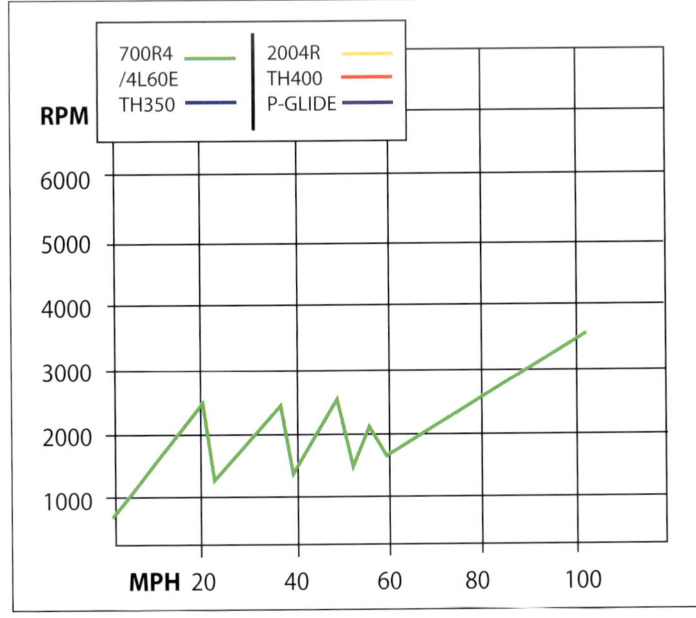

700-R4
The 700-4R and 4L60E have the same gear ratios (3.06:1, 1.63:1, 1.00:1, 0.070:1, so there is no separate chart for the 4L60. The green line at peak represents engine speed at gear upshift under normal throttle.

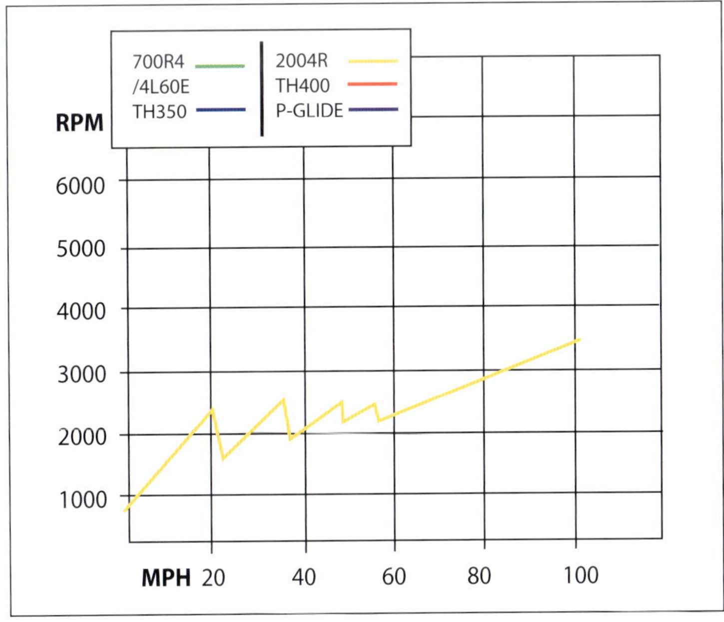

200-4R
Upshift events are represented by the peaks in the continuum. Notice the uniformity of the 200-4R shifts and the "close ratio" of the gear spread.

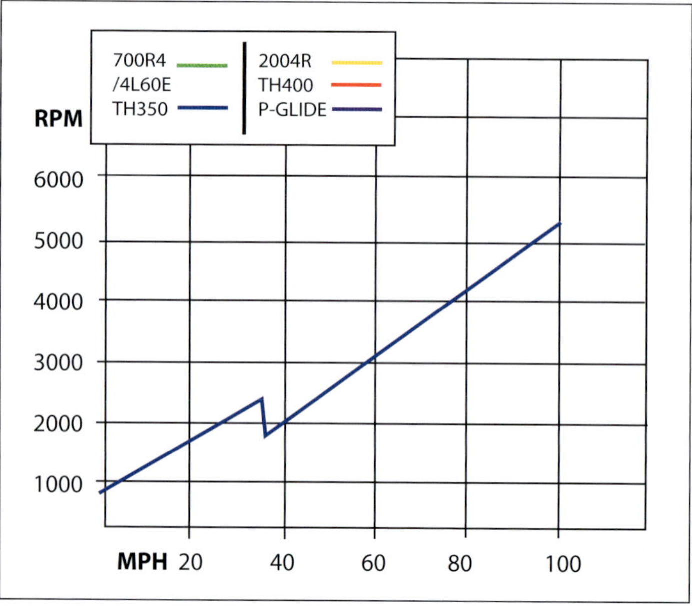

Powerglide
Still a marvel, the 2-speed Powerglide is the choice of racers and streeters alike whose car is equipped with a large displacement engine and/or a power-adder (lots of low end torque). It is available with a 1.76:1 or 1.82:1 Low gear.

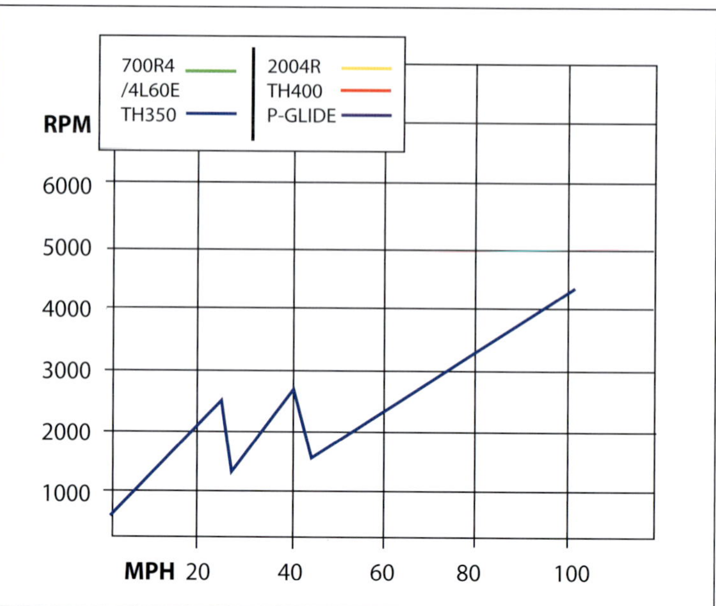

TH350
Call the TH350 old standby number one. Inexpensive and still available in quantity, it is probably the single most used automatic transmission in hot rodding. Ratios: 2.52:1, 1.52:1, and 1:1.

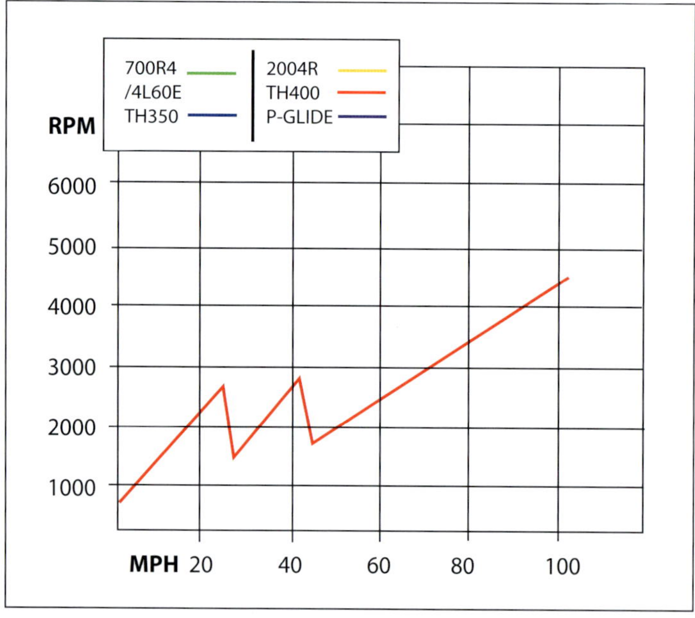

TH400
Inherently a brute, the TH400 is the hands-down pick for a big-block, a big, big-block or lots of power-adder power. Other than the 4L80E, the TH400 is the biggest and heaviest of all the passenger car automatics.

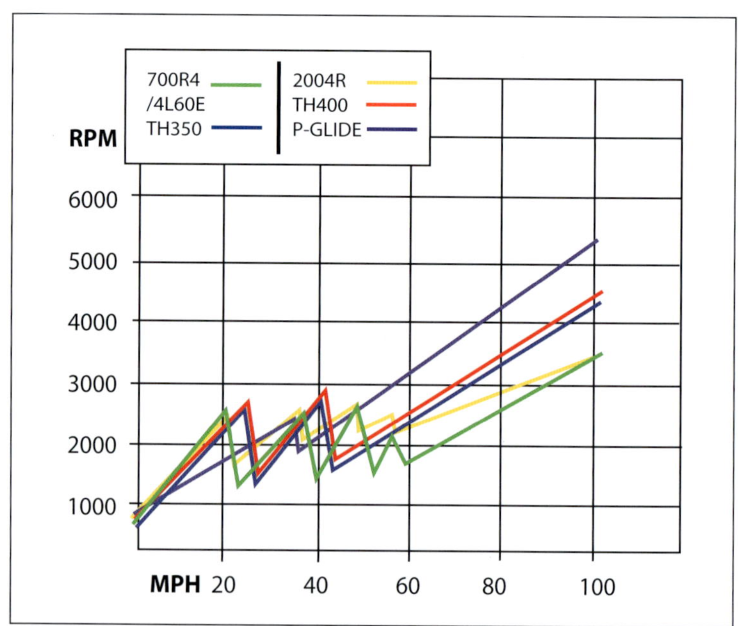

Overlay
Note distinct similarities between the TH350 and TH400 with respect to shift event. On the face of it, the 700-R4 or 4L60E looks to be the ideal ways to pass torque with the most mechanical and fuel-saving efficiency.

Swapper's Source Guide

All items are street or street/strip only, though certain of these manufacturers also build racing versions.

A-1 Transmissions
818-884-6222
www.a-1automatictransmissions.com
TH-350, TH-400, Powerglide transmissions, torque converters

ACC Performance Products Plus, Inc
888-267-7464
www.accperformance.com
TH-350, TH-400, Powerglide, 700R4, 4L60E, 4L80E torque converters

Alto Products Corporation
251-368-7777
www.automatictrans.com
Transmission components

ATI Performance Products
800-284-3433
www.atiracing.com
TH-400, TH-350, 700R4, Powerglide transmissions, torque converters, components, torsional dampers

Art Carr Performance Transmission
888-526-5868
www.artcarr.com
TH-350 transmissions, torque converters, shifters, components for TH-350 and TH-400

ATO Racing Trans and Converter
916-636-3283
Custom-built transmissions

B&M Racing and Performance Products
818-882-6422
www.bmracing.com
TH-400, TH-350, 700R4, 4L60 transmissions, torque converters, shifters, driveline components

Bowler Performance Transmissions
618-943-4856
www.bowlertransmissions.com
200-4R, 4L60E, 4L65E, 700R4, 4L70E (Trailblazer SS), 4L80E, 4L85E transmissions, transmission kits, TV-cable correction kits, paddle shifters, components

California Performance Transmission
800-278-2277
www.cpttransmission.com
200-4R torque converters, components

Campbell Enterprises
804-779-0888
www.campbellenterprises.com
200-R4 torque converters

Coan Engineering
765-456-3957
www.coanracing.com
TH-350, TH-400, 700R4, 4L60E, 4L80E transmissions, torque converters, components

Competition Transmission & Converters
716-692-1901
www.competitiontransmission.com
TH-350, TH-400, 700R4, 4L60, 4L80 transmissions, torque converters, components

Daaco Incorporated
800-443-2226
www.daccoinc.com
Torque converters, components, electronics

Dynamic Racing Transmissions
203-315-0138
www.dynamicracingtrans.com
200-R4, TH-350, TH-400 transmissions, torque converters

Edgar's Transmission
913-299-0987
www.edgarstransmission.com
TH-350, TH-400, 700R4 transmissions

FB Performance Transmissions, Inc.
631-242-0008
www.fbperformance.com
TH-350, TH-400, 200-R4, 700R4, 4L60E, 4L80E transmissions, components

Gearstar Performance Transmissions
800-633-2353
www.gearstar.net
TH-350, TH-400, 22-R4, 700R4, 4L60E, 4L65E, 4L80E transmissions

GM Performance Parts
www.gmperformanceparts.com
4L60E, 4L65E, 4L80E transmissions (includes torque converter), controllers for same

HGM Electronics
310-465-0220
www.hgmelectronics.com
Electronic transmission controllers and ancillaries for 4L60E, 4L65E, 4L80E, 4L85E

Hughes Performance
520-624-4441
www.hughesperformance.com
TH-350, TH400, 4L60, 4L60, 4L60E, 4L80E transmissions, torque converters, components

Jet Performance Products
800-535-1161
www.jetchip.com
4L60E, 4L80E, 700R4 computer-to-non-computer vehicle transmission conversion kits, torque converters, shift kits, programmers, components

Level 10 Performance Transmission Systems Products
973-827-1000
www.levelten.com
Transmissions, torque converters, calibration kits, components

Masta Performance
248-685-8710
www.mastaperformance.com
TH-350, TH-400, Powerglide transmissions, components

Monster Transmission & Performance
800-708-0087
www.eatmyshift.com
TH-350, TH-400, 200R4, 700R4, 4L60E, 4L65E, 4L80E, 6L80E transmissions, torque converters, exterior components, conversion kits

Mike's Transmission
661-723-0081
www.mikestransmission.com
TH-350, TH-400, 700R, Powerglide transmissions, torque converters, components

Munsinger Torque Converters
909-628-0740
www.munsingertorqueconverters.com
Torque converters

Powertrain Control Solutions
804-752-6025
www.powertraincontrolsolutions.com
4L60E, 4L65E, 4L70E 4L80E, 4L85E transmission controllers, data loggers, TPS adapters

Performance Automotive and Transmission Center
888-877-1008
www.transmissioncenter.net
200-4R, 700R4, 4L60E, 4L70E 4L80E, torque converters, components

Performance Torque Converters
256-383-6868
www.ptcrace.com
TH-350, TH-400, torque converters, components

Pro-Tech Transmissions
866-776-8321
www.protechtransmissions.com
Transmissions, torque converters, components

ProTorque Custom Built Torque Converters
631-218-8700
www.protorque.com
Torque converters

R&D Engineering
469-688-6985
www.rd-eng.com
Electric-to-mechanical speedometer kits, 4L80E tail housing kits for same

Reactor Products
310-323-0065
www.reactorproducts.com
Billet aluminum flexplates

Rossler Transmissions, Inc
330-530-5000
www.rosslertrans.com
TH-350, TH-400, 4L60E, 4L80E transmissions

Select Performance
888-557-3532
www.selecttransmissions.com
Transmissions, torque converters, components

Shiftworks
585-383-0574
www.shiftworks.com
Shifters for TH-350, TH-400, 200-4R, 700R4, 4L60, 4L65E, 4L80E, electronic-to mechanical speedometer conversion tail housings for 4L60E, 4L80E

Sonnax Performance
800-463-2600
www.powerglide.com
Torque converters, components

Superior Transmission Parts, Inc
800-451-3115
850-575-7155 (tech)
www.superior-transmission.com
Shift correction kits for 200-4R, TH-350C, TH-400, 700R4, 4L60E, 4L80E

TCI
888-776-9824
www.tciauto.com
TH-350, TH-400, 700R4, 4L60E, 4L80E, 200-4R, 200C transmissions, torque converters, shifters, harmonic balancers, components

TransGo
626-443-7451
www.transgo.com
Shift kits, reprogramming kits, components

Transmission Specialties, Inc.
610-485-9110
www.transmission-specialties.com
TH-350, TH400, 200-4R, 700R4, transmissions, torque converters, components, shifters

Turbo Action, Inc.
904 741-4850
www.turboaction.com
TH350, TH-375, TH-400, 200-4R transmissions, torque converters, shifters, components, controllers

Ultimate Converter Concepts
203-874-2100
www.ultimateconverter.com
Torque converters

Yank Performance Converters
775-826-9955
www.converter.cc
Torque converters

NOTES

NOTES